To Aphrodite, Goddess of Love, in all her incarnatio[...]

Stephanie Jean Clement, Ph.D. (Colorado), holds a doctorate in transpersonal psychology and has practiced astrology for nearly thirty years. Her other books include *Mapping Your Birthchart, Mapping Your Family Relationships, Power of the Midheaven, Charting Your Spiritual Path with Astrology, What Astrology Can Do for You,* and *Dreams: Working Interactive.*

MAPPING YOUR SEX LIFE

Understanding Your Approach
to Passion, Trust & Intimacy

STEPHANIE JEAN CLEMENT, Ph.D.

Llewellyn Publications
St. Paul, Minnesota

First Edition
First Printing, 2005

Book design by Donna Burch
Cover planet images © Digital Vision And Digital Stock
Cover design by Kevin R. Brown
Edited by Andrea Neff
Llewellyn is a registered trademark of Llewellyn Worldwide, Ltd.

Chart wheels were produced by the Kepler program by permission of Cosmic Patterns Software, Inc. (www.AstroSoftware.com)

Library of Congress Cataloging-in-Publication Data

Clement, Stephanie Jean.
    Mapping your sex life / Stephanie Jean Clement.
        p.   cm. — (Astrology made easy series)
    Includes bibliographical references and index.
    ISBN 0-7387-0644-2
      1. Astrology and sex. I. Title. II. Series.

    BF1729.S4C52 2005
    133.5'83067—dc22   2004063318

Llewellyn Publications
A Division of Llewellyn Worldwide, Ltd.
P.O. Box 64383, Dept. 0-7387-0644-2
St. Paul, MN 55164-0383, U.S.A.
www.llewellyn.com

Printed in the United States of America

Other Books by Stephanie Jean Clement, Ph.D.

Charting Your Career
(1999)

Dreams: Working Interactive (with Terry Lee Rosen)
(2000)

What Astrology Can Do for You
(2000)

Charting Your Spiritual Path with Astrology
(2001)

Civilization Under Attack (editor and contributor)
(2001)

Power of the Midheaven
(2001)

Meditation for Beginners
(2002)

Meditación para principiantes
(2002)

Mapping Your Birthchart
(2003)

Mapping Your Family Relationships
(2004)

Forthcoming Books by Stephanie Jean Clement, Ph.D.

Chart Patterns
(2006)

Acknowledgments

Carl and Sandra Weschcke, and David and Fei Cochrane, shared my vision for the *Astrology Made Easy* series and for this book. Without them, this book and program would not have been possible.

As usual, Andrea Neff and Donna Burch have taken my writing and turned it into a book I am proud to have authored.

Nancy Mostad has offered her support throughout the publishing process, ever since I first sent in an idea for a book years ago. I value her friendship and her insights.

There are too many astrologers to mention here. Joyce Wehrman was a teacher who facilitated thinking, as well as study, about astrology. She provided me with the best foundation I could have wanted for astrological writing and counseling.

Sarah Cooper invited me into the community of astrologers early in my career, and always made me feel welcome.

Thanks to my friends Judy Rosen, Catherine Linnane, Gina Kolbe, and Kris Brandt Riske.

I also thank my husband Greg, who, by the way, has *not* read this book, and my children, who don't *even* want to read this book!

Contents

Ten

Eleven

Twelve

Thirteen

Fourteen

Fifteen

Sixteen

Charts

Chart data for Mata Hari came from AstroDatabank (www.astrodatabank.com).

Introduction

Sometimes it isn't about love. Or perhaps I should say it isn't *just* about love. You have physical desires, and you want to find ways to satisfy those desires. Everyone grows up with all sorts of fantasies about the perfect lover and the perfect physical chemistry. We have come to expect these fantasies to be satisfied by the person with whom we fall in love, and it isn't always the perfect bliss we anticipated.

Astrology is able to examine every area of your life. Your sex life is no exception. Through understanding your own desires and how they fit into your fantasies, you learn how to ask your partner to meet your needs. You can also take a look at your partner's astrology chart to see what his or her fantasies and needs are all about. The two of you can create a whole new level of passion by understanding how your desires are similar— and different.

The goal of this book is to use astrology to inform you about the myriad desires, needs, and expectations people have where sexuality is concerned. You will learn that the way you were taught as a child or teen is definitely not all there is to your physical passion. You will probably find out that what you work out logically is not totally satisfying. You may even discover keys to your own pleasure that you never suspected. You will certainly learn to appreciate the differences between you and your partner, and how to play (not work) with each other's fantasies and desires.

Imagine having twelve different approaches to sexual thoughts, feelings, and expression. Then imagine having twelve different ways to implement each of those expressions. Then imagine combining your 144 varieties with those of your partner. Your sex life just improved by over 2,000 percent! Astrology can help you discover subtleties you never knew existed.

So get a glass of your favorite wine (or soda), a few snacks, and this book. Get cozy and warm, and begin your voyage of discovery as you map your sex life in all of its many manifestations. Your physical pleasure will never be the same!

1
The Basics of Astrology

This book is written for people who want to improve their sex lives. It's for people who believe that sex, like any other activity, should be rich in meaning. Astrology provides a model for your entire life—your potential, the way you work with the energies surrounding you, and the direction of your life in the future. Thus astrology also provides a definitive picture of what your sex life could be like.

Throughout this book I refer to the "partner." This is for the sake of verbal convenience. Your partner could be male, female, a spiritual being, or even yourself.

The CD-ROM that comes with this book creates a birth chart, and also an interpretation. The program performs all the mathematical calculations, based on the birth date, time, and place. The result is a two-dimensional "map" of where all the planets were in the zodiac at the time for which the chart was created.

I will examine the birth chart for Mata Hari (chart 1), a woman whose name is synonymous with sex. Now, just because Mata Hari was a sex symbol does not mean that her chart reveals the ideal planetary arrangement for a satisfying sex life. By the same token, you are unlikely to become an international spy, using your sexual wiles to attract the people who have information you want. Mata Hari's story is rich with imagery and feeling, and may be a fantasy that piques your sexual interest. I use this example to introduce the astrological factors we will be looking at throughout the book, and to show how sex was an integral part of Mata Hari's chart, and of her life.

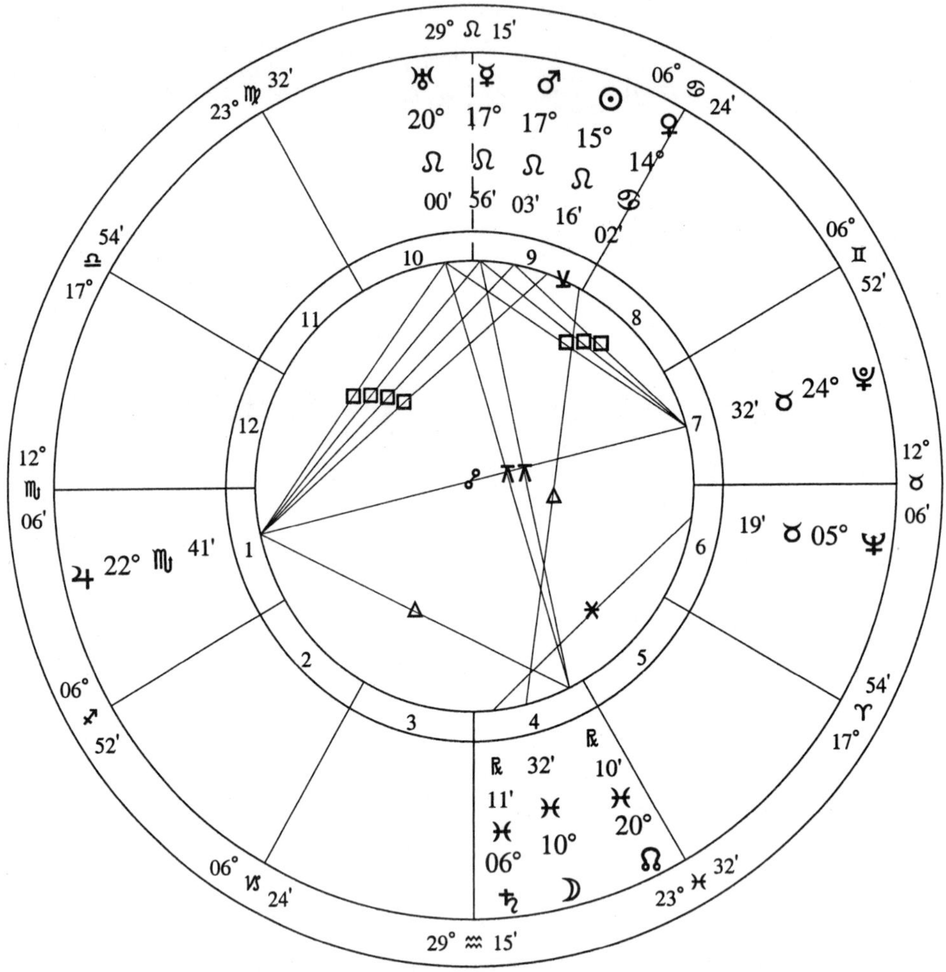

Chart 1: Mata Hari
August 7, 1876 / Leeuwarden, Netherlands / 1:00 PM LMT
Koch Houses

Notice that part of Mata Hari's chart is full of planets, while several sections of the circle (houses) are empty. Each chart you look at will have a different arrangement of information. Empty houses simply indicate areas of life that are less dominant or interesting to the individual, while occupied houses show where the person's attention is likely to be focused. There are many components in a birth chart, and I will introduce them in this chapter.

Can't wait to create your own chart? Then turn to appendix 2 for instructions on how to use the CD-ROM. There you will find step-by-step directions on how to recreate Mata Hari's chart. To create your own chart, just insert data for yourself to replace her birth date, time, and place.

Chart Components

The main parts of the astrological chart are the signs, planets, houses, and aspects. The planets signify who or what is active in our lives, the signs tell us how each planet is acting, and the houses tell us where in life the action takes place. The relationships between the planets are the aspects. The lines in the center of the circle connect planets and points that are in aspect to each other (planets that are connected in significant ways). The symbol on each line indicates the aspect involved.

Signs

Let's take the signs first. On the left side of the chart form, there is a list of names and glyphs (symbols) for each zodiac sign. Each sign represents a particular psychological need, reflected in certain tendencies within the personality.

Sign	Symbol	Psychological Need
Aries	♈	To be self-confident and free; to lead
Taurus	♉	To be resourceful and productive
Gemini	♊	To communicate
Cancer	♋	To give and receive emotional warmth and security
Leo	♌	To create; to express oneself
Virgo	♍	To analyze and find order

Sign	Symbol	Psychological Need
Libra	♎	To create harmony and balance
Scorpio	♏	To experience intense emotional transformation
Sagittarius	♐	To explore and expand horizons
Capricorn	♑	To find structure and receive social acknowledgment
Aquarius	♒	To innovate; to be original; to be unconventional
Pisces	♓	To gain faith and belief in transcendence

Everyone has all twelve signs in their chart, and therefore everyone's chart reflects these needs somewhere in their life. When you talk about your own sign, you are referring to the place where your Sun is. Mata Hari had the Sun in the sign of Leo (♌). Usually you need only the birth date to determine the Sun sign. For the days when the Sun changes signs, you need to know the birth time as well.

You can see from the list that some signs seem more conducive to sex than others. Not to worry—there is plenty of depth to each Sun sign, and there are plenty of other factors to consider in your chart too.

Houses

The second factor to consider is the houses (chart 2). The twelve houses represent the different activities and experiences we encounter throughout our lives. The numbers around the inner circle of the chart indicate which house is which. The cusp of each house is the first edge, going in a counterclockwise direction. The First House is always just below the horizon (the horizontal line on the left side of the circle). The cusp of the First House is called the Ascendant. There are signs on both cusps of each house, and sometimes there is a whole sign inside a house, called an *intercepted* sign. In Mata Hari's chart you can see the symbol for Scorpio (♏) on the left side of the chart (on the Ascendant), and the symbol for Taurus (♉) on the right side of the chart (at the Descendant, the cusp of the Seventh House).

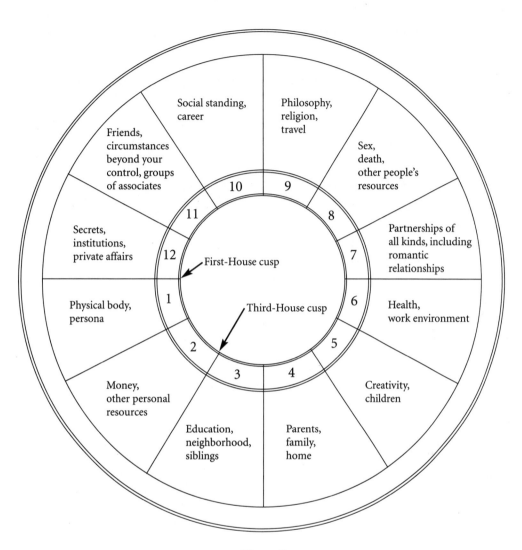

Chart 2
The Houses

House	Experience
1	Physical body, persona
2	Money and other personal resources
3	Education, neighborhood, siblings
4	Parents, family, home
5	Children, creativity
6	Health, work environment
7	Partnerships of all kinds, including romantic relationships
8	Sex, death, other people's resources
9	Religion, travel, philosophy
10	Career, social standing
11	Friends, groups of associates, circumstances beyond your control
12	Private affairs, secrets, institutions

Looking at Mata Hari's chart, you might expect to find something in the Eighth House of sex, death, and other people's resources. After all, her life was focused intensely on sex. Yet there are no planets there. Instead there are five planets in the Ninth House! This tells us two things, the first of which is that Mata Hari's life was focused very strongly on Ninth-House matters. We know that she traveled a great deal, and we suspect that religion was not a strong focus for her, although she used religion as a backdrop for her sexual performances The second thing to note is that other chart indications can be very important where sex is concerned.

The Sun's House

The time of day at which you were born determines the house placement of the Sun and the arrangement of the signs within the houses in your birth chart. The twelve signs of the zodiac rise and set during each twenty-four-hour period, just as the Sun does. Each sign moves across the Midheaven (the middle of the sky) in about two hours, and a different sign rises in the east (the left part of the chart) in the same time period. The Midheaven is at the top of the chart, and the Ascendant, or *rising sign,* is on the left side at the horizon line. The signs are shown in the outside ring of the chart wheel at the lines (cusps) that indicate the beginning of each house.

The Sun rises at dawn in the east, at the Ascendant (First-House cusp), and is on the Descendant (Seventh-House cusp) at about sunset. The Midheaven (Tenth-House cusp) is the noon point in the chart. If the Sun is there in a chart, the birth time is close to noon. The IC, or *Imum Coeli* (the Fourth-House cusp), at the bottom of the chart represents midnight and is opposite the Midheaven.

By locating the Sun in the chart wheel, you can estimate the time of birth. Mata Hari was born at 1:00 PM in the summer, so we know the Sun (☉) will be past the Midheaven (the highest point) in the chart. Her Sun is in the Ninth House. The signs rise in a clockwise motion at the rate of about 15 degrees each hour, and Mata Hari's Sun is about 14 degrees past the Midheaven, so we know that the Sun was at the Midheaven about one hour before she was born. The Sun appears where you expect to find it in the twenty-four-hour wheel of the chart, based on the birth time.

The Sun's Sign

What does the sign on each house cusp tell us? If the sign represents a psychological need and the house represents an area of life, then the sign on a house tells us which needs tend to be strongly associated within that particular area of human experience. Everyone has the same needs, but we express them in very individual ways, based upon where the signs are located in the houses. This is a profound truth to be explored through astrology. If you never do anything else with astrology, understanding your own needs in terms of the signs and houses in your birth chart will be a powerful tool in your life. The same holds true for your family and friends. If you understand their needs more clearly, you will be able to help them and have compassion for them.

The Sun sign is what people mean when they ask, "What's your sign?" Mata Hari is a Leo—she has the Sun (☉) in the sign of Leo (♌) in the Ninth House of her birth chart. By looking at the tables in this chapter for basic planet, sign, and house meanings, we find that her psychological need is to express herself (Leo ♌), and the area where this need is expressed is religion, travel, and philosophy (Ninth House).

What does this mean? We can anticipate that Mata Hari will find a way to incorporate travel, religion, and philosophy into her life. She will not be a stay-at-home person. She will soak up philosophical thoughts wherever she goes. Because she has four other planets in the Ninth House along with her Sun, she will focus a lot of energy on her desire to experience the world.

Planets

The Sun, Moon, and planets represent the parts of our being. They also indicate people who come into our lives—people who have the characteristics of the planet and the sign in which the planet is found. The symbols and names of the planets are listed at the lower right part of the chart form, and the house placements of the planets are listed at the bottom center of the form (and in chart 3). The following table includes the symbols for the planets and a few words about the part of the personality that each planet reflects.

Planet	Associated Sign(s)	Part of the Personality	People or Things in the Environment
☉ Sun	♌ Leo	Expression, individuality	Men, leaders, daytime
☽ Moon	♋ Cancer	Feelings and habits	Women, nighttime, the masses
☿ Mercury	♊ Gemini	Communication style	Students or teachers
	♍ Virgo	Analysis, service	Employers, coworkers
♀ Venus	♉ Taurus,	Value system	Women, beautiful things
	♎ Libra	Social attraction	Partners, opponents
♂ Mars	♈ Aries	Desire and action, energy	Men, sharp things
♃ Jupiter	♐ Sagittarius	The process of expansion	Religious or legal people, big things
♄ Saturn	♑ Capricorn	Structure, responsibility	Police, cautious people, detailed things
♅ Uranus	♒ Aquarius	Intuition, ritual, sudden change	Unusual people, anything new
♆ Neptune	♓ Pisces	Receptivity, imagination	Sensitive people, strange things
♇ Pluto	♏ Scorpio	Power and will	Organizations, forceful people
Ascendant	ASC	Persona, physical body	
Midheaven	MC	Self-awareness, achievement	

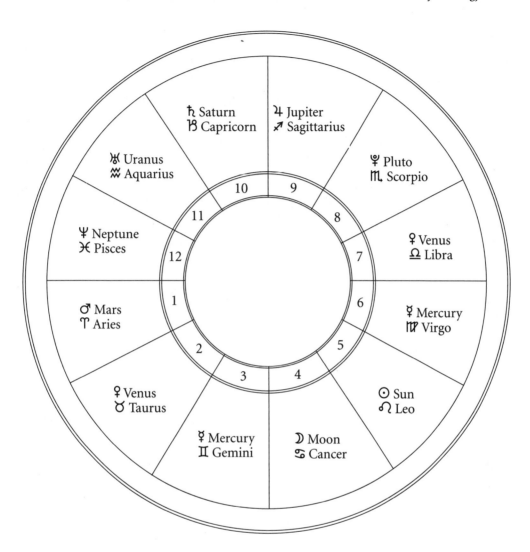

Chart 3
Astrological Associations of the Planets and Signs

Aspects

The fourth factor in chart interpretation is the aspects—the distance between the planets in a particular chart. Certain harmonic relationships—divisions of the 360-degree circle by whole numbers—have been found to be significant in charts. Some astrologers consider a wide range of aspects, and others stick to just a few. Chart 4 shows the aspects in a chart wheel. Traditional astrologers use only the conjunction, opposition, trine, square, and sextile.

Aspect	Symbol	Harmonic	Exact Number of Degrees	Meaning	Orb Allowed
Conjunction	☌	360	0	Beginning and ending	6
Opposition	☍	2	180	Awareness	6
Trine	△	3	120	Comfort	6
Square	□	4	90	Challenge	6
Sextile	✳	6	60	Opportunity	6
Quintile	Q	5	72	Talent and creativity	3
Septile	⑦	7	51.2	Fate	2
Semisquare	∠	8	45	Tension	2
Semisextile	⊻	12	30	Growth	2
Biquintile	Bq	5	144	Creativity	3
Sesquisquare	⟎	8	135	Agitation	2
Quincunx	⚻	12	150	Adjustment	2

In this book I have categorized the aspects into three general groups:

- Challenging aspects (conjunction, square, opposition)
- Constructive aspects (trine, sextile, quintile, biquintile)
- Zingers (semisextile, quincunx, semisquare, sesquisquare)

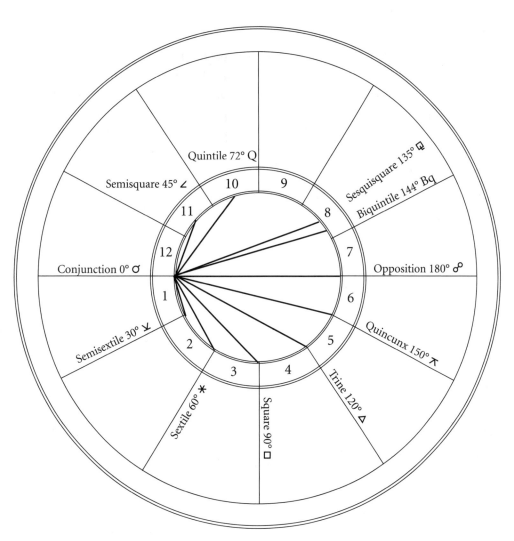

Chart 4
Aspects

The challenging aspects are "in your face" connections where your sex life is concerned. They force you to look at any issues that arise. The constructive aspects support your quest for sexual satisfaction. They indicate conditions you find appealing, opportunities to find satisfaction, and areas of creativity. The zingers indicate areas where you surprise or even shock yourself with your reactions. These aspects indicate areas of less conscious awareness where impulses and feelings arise out of nowhere. They also indicate areas where personal growth can occur, and where you may potentially find profound sexual pleasure.

The chart itself contains 360 degrees. The conjunction aspect occurs when two planets are exactly together in the same degree. Mata Hari has Mercury (☿) very close to Mars (♂) in her chart, so they are said to be conjunct. The same is true for Venus (♀) and the Sun (☉), even though they are about 1 degree apart. Each planet has an *orb* of influence—the planets need to be within only a few degrees of orb to form an aspect. Note the aspect symbols and orbs on your chart printout in the lower left corner of the form, as well as in the previous table.

In our example, Mata Hari has Mercury (☿) and Mars (♂) close together in the Ninth House in Leo (Mercury is at 17 degrees 56 minutes Leo, and Mars is at 17 degrees 03 minutes Leo). They are within 1 degree of an exact conjunction. Her need to be creative and to express herself (Leo ♌) is centered on travel (Ninth House). Her communication style (Mercury ☿) and her desire and energy (Mars ♂) are closely united (conjunction ♂) in fulfilling this need. Does this make sense when we look at Mata Hari's life? Realistically, we can speculate about her life, but we are limited by what history has recorded about her, and generally we see her in terms of her career as a spy. However, we can say that Mata Hari created situations in which she could travel and engage in intense verbal and sexual communication with males. Now we begin to see the focus on sexuality in her chart! In the next chapter we will look at her whole chart for more indicators.

Each chapter of this book will expand on the ideas presented in this chapter, showing how each planet, sign, house, and aspect reveals details about your sex life. The book is organized around topics related to sexuality. You will learn that most, if not all, parts of your chart indicate something about your sex life.

The individual aspects are described in chapter 15 of this book. Once you have printed your chart, you can see what aspects each planet makes, and then read about them. Most of us have quirks that we don't fully grasp. As you read the aspect interpretations, you will begin to understand your complex sexual makeup better.

Exercise

Using your own chart or that of a friend, look at each symbol. You may want to make an extra copy of the chart for this exercise.

- Write the name of each sign next to its symbol in the chart.
- Write the name of each planet next to its symbol.
- Look at the aspects in the center of the chart wheel, and notice which planets are closely associated with each other.
- Using the keywords in this chapter, make a list for each planet. First list the words for the planet, then the words for the sign, and then the words for the house.
- Now, using some of these words, make up sentences that describe your sexual energy, as I have done for Mata Hari.
- Notice how these sentences fit (or don't fit) what you know about your sex life and your sexual desires.
- Adjust the sentences by using different words.

When you have finished, you will have your first, very basic look at a portrait of your sex life!

Summary

In the following chapters, we will explore each planet, sign, house, and aspect in greater detail. You may find it helpful to memorize the symbols and keywords for each of them, so that you have a basic concept of each factor in your chart. Remember, we are focusing on sexuality. The planets, signs, houses, and aspects have a much broader significance in your life, so you may want to consider how other factors affect your sexuality as you read through each chapter.

To give you a taste of how astrology reveals your sexuality, the next chapter offers a complete analysis of Mata Hari's chart. You have seen what just a little bit of information can tell you. Now get a feel for an overall chart analysis from the sexual perspective, and learn more about this twentieth-century legend of sex and intrigue.

2
Mata Hari
Sex and Intrigue

You say you want more excitement and intrigue in your sex life? Mata Hari had one husband (she divorced him) and multiple lovers who fulfilled her every need. She became an exotic dancer and insinuated herself into the highest levels of French society, and eventually became a double agent during World War I. She was tried as a spy and executed, even though there is significant doubt about her actual espionage efforts.

You say you don't want your sex life to be quite that exciting? Not willing to be executed? You may still find some interesting facts in Mata Hari's story that you can apply to your own life. One doesn't have to face a firing squad to have a richly passionate sexual life.

Mata Hari's name is synonymous with sexual intrigue and betrayal. Her actions as a spy during World War I were directly responsible for extensive loss of life and almost certainly delayed the end of the war. Her biography indicates that her sexual exploits spanned the boundaries of several European nations, and included men on the French, German, and Russian fronts. Her sheer audacity in a time following the reserved Victorian era may not seem that impressive by today's standards. As you read, keep in mind the position of women in early twentieth-century Europe, the social values, and the obstacles to travel and relocation at that time. In this context, Mata Hari's accomplishments were highly unusual, to say the least.

Mata Hari's Chart

Sun in Leo

Mata Hari was certainly demonstrative. She used her sexuality as a tool, even as a weapon. Action was the only thing that kept her life interesting. She was also determined—determined to have a lot of money so she could buy everything she wanted, and determined to make people love her and want her.

She was consistent, too, within her own logic. She could be counted on to do something more original, more outrageous, or more deadly. She wanted to rub shoulders with the elite, and she married a British aristocrat who took her to live in the Far East. She might have stayed with him if he had not been a drinker. However, Mata Hari wanted the dominant position, and she may never have been able to be the dominant partner in that relationship. She used her sexuality to establish her position, and to maintain it with many different lovers.

I said elsewhere in this book that a Leo Sun may reflect selfishness. Mata Hari demonstrated selfishness in just about everything she did. Even her stage name made her the center of everything. Mata Hari means "the light of the day," or "the eye of the day." I have also mentioned that the Ninth-House Sun is restless. Mata Hari lived in several countries on two continents, traveling from one country to another with little thought for her own future. She was always able to find a way to set herself up with another man and use her body for profit. She danced her way into the hearts of the Paris elite, supposedly performing a sacred dance of Shiva while actually doing a striptease.

Mercury in Leo

Mata Hari was the heart and soul of enthusiasm when it came to sex. She could make any partner feel wonderful. She may not have treated her sexual partners as possessions, but she certainly treated them as objects. I mentioned that Mercury in Leo needs to cultivate loyalty. Ultimately, the lack of loyalty was Mata Hari's downfall.

Mercury in the Ninth House is the second indicator of her footloose ways. She was exotic in ways that don't come across well in pictures. She used costuming and sinuous movement to cover what was lacking in authenticity and dance training. She also was

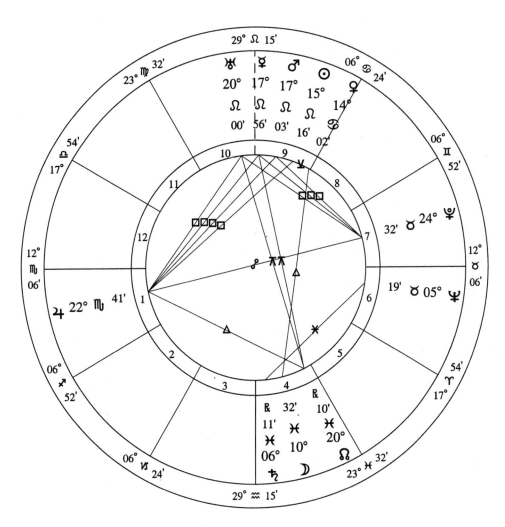

Chart 5: Mata Hari
August 7, 1876 / Leeuwarden, Netherlands / 1:00 PM LMT
Koch Houses

apparently able to turn on a dime, one minute removing veils in her dance, and the next minute dressed just like the rest of the ladies and sipping tea or a drink with them.

Moon in Pisces

So what did Mata Hari need? She needed the sympathy of her audience. She needed people to see her as noble, elegant, and, most of all, sexy. She needed to engage in sex. Like most people, she would get the full enjoyment of sex through surrender. Her biography indicates that she acted as though she surrendered only to get what she wanted. She would say to a lover, "You may do with me what you wish," and later she would say of that lover, "I conquered him" or "I can do with him whatever I want."[1] Her stock in trade was seduction and *apparent* submission.

The Fourth-House Moon suggests that home and family were important to her, and they were, but not in the usual sense. She would start out in a hotel, and then take a lover. This happened many times in her career. She spent lavishly to furnish her nest, wherever it was.

Neptune in Taurus in the Sixth House

Mata Hari experienced cyclical ups and downs in her career. She latched on to her husband very tightly, only to leave him. She went to Paris with hardly any money, and made good almost immediately. She would be thrown out of one situation and thrown into another. There is little evidence that she used drugs on a regular basis. That would have hastened her downfall.

Mata Hari had sexual magnetism in remarkable abundance. She was able to transport her partners to new levels of pleasure. She could have experienced deep satisfaction in marriage to the right person. Her material goals and selfish nature were not compatible, however, with long-term relationships.

Scorpio Ascendant

Read any Sun sign astrology book, and you will discover that Scorpio is the sign of sex and death. When Scorpio is on the Ascendant, the person has multiple options for how to express sexual energy. Mata Hari made the most of those options to create her entire life and career. For example, on her second move to Paris, she arrived with hardly any money, checked into the Grand Hotel, and immediately acquired a wealthy lover.[2] He was happy to pay her bills and purchase a wardrobe. With that move to France, she decided to start at the top instead of working her way up.

Her first foray into the world of exotic dancing was at a private party. Draped in veils, she performed her "Temple Dance," and enthralled the audience. She removed the veils one by one, leaving only a metallic bra and what we might call a jeweled G-string. This fits what the books say about Scorpio to a T. Minutes after completing her dance, she would reappear, dressed just like all the other ladies, to drink champagne. The prim and proper look is also associated with Scorpio, a sign of extremes.

Jupiter in Scorpio
Mata Hari lived a life of extraordinary sexual excess. For her, more sex was better, and too much was never enough. Her greed for material comforts of all kinds was met through sexual means.

Taurus Descendant
What was Mata Hari looking for in a partner? In a word, money. She wanted money, luxury, and security. The first two she managed fairly easily, but the third was to elude her. None of the men who so willingly paid her way were willing to marry her, although one did set her up in a country mansion in 1910 (she had obtained a divorce from her less than satisfactory husband in 1906).[3]

Pluto in Taurus
Mata Hari's downfall was a practical yet ruthless Frenchman. He played her skillfully and probably lied or exaggerated her role as a spy, although everyone apparently believed that the Germans paid her to spy during World War I.

Leo Midheaven
Her biographer states that Mata Hari had an introspective, ego-conscious side. She paid attention to Eastern religions while she was in Indonesia with her first husband. She incorporated those religious motifs into her exotic dancing. She never quite understood the differences between Buddhism, the religion of Indonesia, where she had lived, and Hinduism. While much of her dance technique was Indonesian, Hinduism offered the

greater focus on sexuality, which she liked. She discovered the Vedantic tradition, and understood that life was an illusion.

Aquarius on the Fourth-House Cusp

The wellspring of her inspiration was rebellion. She never seemed to quite fit within all the boundaries of society, no matter where she went. She said she remained emotionally uninvolved with her lovers. Her dancing was a paradoxical blending of submission and seduction.

Mars in Leo in the Ninth House

Mata Hari traveled to the Orient to be with her husband, and later traveled all over Europe. She had plenty of energy to pursue sex and men wherever she found the opportunity. The sexual side of Mars' energy came through emphatically in her zest for excitement with new and different men.

Venus in Cancer in the Ninth House

When we look beyond the surface of her many affairs and her exotic dancing career, we discover that Mata Hari was idealistic where her actual love life was concerned. She hardened herself to her many lovers, but she did finally fall in love with a Russian officer, and cared for him after he was wounded. Throughout her life she also demonstrated the desire to have a lovely home, filled with people she could depend on.

Pisces on the Fifth-House Cusp

Pisces on the Fifth-House cusp indicates that Mata Hari was capable of giving. She was empathetic enough to divine her lovers' sexual needs, and then fulfill them. In addition, the Moon in Pisces in the Fourth House confirms that she also needed to be needed.

She did have one lover she cared for after he was injured and gassed by the Germans. He turned out to be very expensive. Very late in the game, Mata Hari sent a lot of money to her Russian lover, money that she could well have used for her own defense.

Virgo on the Eleventh-House Cusp

How did Mata Hari evaluate the "love received" from her many conquests? She did so based on Virgo-style accounting. She wanted the best of everything, and evaluated any expression of love on the basis of the material return. The single exception to this rule was Masloff, her last lover. He did not shower her with money. In fact, he turned the tables on her, taking money and favors from her.

Gemini on the Eighth-House Cusp

Mata Hari's life gave special meaning to the concept of multiple sexual relationships. It's not that there were no other women in her circles doing the same thing. It's more that she was so brazenly dismissive of the danger in her career as a spy. However, she reportedly made very good money in the spy business, which she used to maintain her lifestyle as a courtesan.

Libra on the Twelfth-House Cusp

Throughout her life, Mata Hari longed for love. She withheld it, so she said, from all her lovers except the last. She demonstrated an amazing lack of moderation. She had to have the best shoes, the best clothes, the best home, and the best partner. When she didn't, she would go out and make the necessary changes. She was both seducible and seductive.

Aspects in Mata Hari's Chart

Saturn Sextile Neptune

It would seem that no opportunity for seduction escaped Mata Hari. At the same time, she had every chance to delude herself about her position. She never seemed to quite believe that she would be caught, and if caught, tried and executed.

Mercury Conjunct Mars

She had a silver tongue. Languages came easily to her, and she was able to fit into French society easily. She apparently did well enough to understand the Germans she spied for, too, and English was also no problem.

Sun Conjunct Mars

Mata Hari was able to act out her fantasies and implement her plans with equal skill. She had a red-hot aura that drew people to her. Mata Hari willingly put tremendous effort into her life, especially her sex life.

Jupiter Opposite Pluto

Here is a hint of the danger that seemed to attract Mata Hari like a moth to a flame. She seemed to relish being on the edge—her dancing was certainly edgy enough for the times. She loved having a brush with the authorities. Toward the end she may have wondered why her sexual tactics didn't work on her judges. The danger lay in the fact that she was willing to risk—and lose—everything.

Mercury Conjunct Uranus

Intuition was a key talent for Mata Hari. She always seemed to know where to go and what to do to make her next conquest. She was the talk of Paris and all of Europe. She knew just how far to go with her dramatic performances.

Sun Conjunct Mercury

She had enough common sense to manage on almost no money when she had to (although sometimes she failed to exercise it).

Jupiter Square Uranus

She was wildly lucky.

Mars Conjunct Uranus

In the end she ran out of luck. What she had left was the nerve to stand before her firing squad with disdain.

Moon Trine Venus

Mata Hari was not fabulously beautiful, nor was her figure extraordinary. She made up for these limitations with her flair for the dramatic and her ability to impress an audience of one or many with her exotic movements and sexual receptiveness.

Moon Conjunct Saturn

The key to Mata Hari's lifestyle was her self-control. She could make do with very little. When she had a lot, she spent it with seeming abandon. Beneath the surface there was a shrewd, calculating mind at work all the time.

Did She Achieve Sexual Satisfaction?

Mata Hari lived a life of action and pleasure. She wanted luxurious clothes and status in society, but above all she wanted action. She was always seeking something new to stimulate her. Because of her life as a courtesan, she didn't really seek to satisfy herself sexually. Instead she sought to control her partners. Her self-control prevented her from achieving ultimate satisfaction.

Throughout this book, you will read about the difference between control and surrender where sex is concerned. To be in control means that you cannot open to the full experience of sexual pleasure. Mata Hari filled the void left by the lack of sexual satisfaction by seeking material pleasures of every kind. Toward the end of her life, Mata Hari found a worthy partner. In doing so, she may have surprised herself. It certainly was out of character compared to the rest of her exploits.

Even though you probably wouldn't want to follow in Mata Hari's footsteps completely, you can take a page from her book on how to stimulate desire in your partner. Even though she was not all that attractive, she was able to dress up in exotic costumes, act out the physical desire of her Dance of Shiva, and attract men to her with ease. What can you add to your repertoire to spice up your sex life? Read on.

----

1. Russell Warren Howe, *Mata Hari: The True Story* (New York: Dodd, Mead & Co., 1986) p. 40.

2. Ibid., p. 34.

3. Ibid., p. 45.

3
The Sun
Physical Needs and Desires

We all have physical needs and desires. Even before we are born, our bodies demand nourishment and pleasure. Pictures of unborn fetuses show them sucking their thumbs, and we know that unborn babies respond to touch and sound. Often mothers speak of the nature of the unborn child as if it were already out in the world. One will squirm around tentatively, while another will kick abruptly and vigorously. Still another will press out in two or three directions at the same time, seemingly trying to make more room for itself.

As soon as the infant enters the world and becomes independent of the mother's body, it expresses its needs through movement and sound. The squirmer may wiggle and nestle into the mother's body while being fed. The kicker will scoot around in bed more than you would think possible for a newborn. The presser will rest with arms and legs extended, as if relishing the abundance of space outside the mother's womb. From these early beginnings, we each experience physical desires, and strive to fulfill them.

Sexually we respond in much the same way. We discover sensual urges and find ways to fulfill our desires. Sometimes we are able to satisfy our own needs, and sometimes we need a partner to truly feel complete.

Among the attributes of your personality and drive indicated by the Sun is your most basic approach to sensual satisfaction. The Sun's position by sign and house, and the aspects it makes to other planets in the chart, provide the basic terrain of your sexual life.

The Sun is associated with love. There are many faces of love that we will not be exploring in this book—love of family, God, country, and love of our work once we find our mission in life. This book considers love given and received through sexual relationships. You are at your best when you give love through patience and kindness. You are not demanding of your partner, and you support him or her through good times and bad. The Bible says that love rejoices in the right, bears all things, hopes all things, endures all things, and never ends. Love is not jealous, arrogant, rude, irritable, or resentful, and love never rejoices in wrong action. Love does not insist on its own way or boast about its experience.

I wish I could say that I live up to this standard in my life. I don't know many people who do. We all have weaknesses and flaws. Sexual relationships tend, in fact, to bring out those flaws so we can identify them and work on them. You may have noticed a few things on the good side that you are able to manifest most of the time. You have probably also noticed a flaw or two that have come up in your sexual relationships.

The above lists offer guidelines for the best and worst that love has to offer. Sexuality, at its best, manifests the strengths of love and minimizes the weaknesses. As relationships deepen over time, we hope that love will grow. If you find yourself in a relationship that does not develop and grow, you may want to look at your own motivations and those of your partner. Perhaps the two of you have very different needs and desires, and these factors are taking you in different directions. Beyond the physical satisfaction of sexual passion, perhaps you see love differently.

There are multiple facets to your sexuality. That's a given. We will begin by examining your sexuality from an individual perspective. While most of us associate sexuality with a partner, in reality we each possess our own individual sexual signature.

At the physical level, partners may have very different expectations. These needs and desires are reflected by the Sun in each person's chart. The Sun represents the life force within you. Its position in the chart reveals something about the heat and energy within you, and also reflects your desire nature.

The Sun in the Elements

Astrologers use the terms fire, earth, air, and water to describe four basic approaches to life. These are comparable to Carl Jung's four personality types: intuition, sensation, thinking, and feeling, respectively.

Sun in the Fire Element

You are basically a demonstrative person. Your energy is visible to others through action and even aggression. You tend to be impulsive about sex. Freedom is essential if you are to bloom into a sexually satisfied being. You are idealistic about partners. You bring your spirit into your sexual life.

Sun in the Earth Element

You are a fundamentally practical person, and practicality extends to your perceptions about your sex life. You want a persistent partner who is willing to keep going until you are satisfied. You tend to be possessive of your partner(s) and somewhat secretive where sexuality is concerned.

Sun in the Air Element

You rely on your capacity to think things through. When you spend too much time thinking about your sex life, though, you find that you never get past the thought stage! Your logical mind is best used in devising a plan for your sex life. Then set logic aside and enjoy the process.

Sun in the Water Element

Emotional experience provides your foundation. Sexuality, for you, is not just about the physical experience. You want emotional satisfaction and you desire a soul mate who understands your depth of feeling. You tend to absorb all kinds of energy from your environment, so you must discriminate in your choice of partners.

The Sun in the Modes

Astrologers also describe three basic methods or modes of dealing with life: cardinal, fixed, and mutable. For each element, there is a sign that uses each mode of approach.

Sun in a Cardinal Sign (direct)

You tend to take the initiative in many areas of your life, so you probably will want to initiate most sexual activities too. You are willing to try new methods, and your enthusiasm can infect your partner. You experience sex in the present moment for the most part. This means that you bring less old business along with you to the bedroom. The best sex for you includes both physical and mental tension.

Sun in a Fixed Sign (stable)

You are a determined person. This affects your physical desires in that you keep searching for the most satisfaction you can give and receive. You like consistency, and therefore may not have your best sex in unusual circumstances. Your power reserves allow you to keep going for hours when the setting is right. You are nothing if not thorough in your exploration of physical pleasure.

Sun in a Mutable Sign (flexible)

Adaptable could be your middle name. You are willing to go with the sexual flow, as long as you are satisfied mentally. You spend a lot of mental energy on the future. This means that good sex includes the potential for future encounters with the same partner. One-night stands, while intriguing, lack the capacity to fully satisfy you. You may enjoy exotic sexual postures.

The Sun in the Signs

Sun in Aries (cardinal fire)

Urgency marks your sexual activities, especially at first. You want it all, and you want it now. Then you often find you want more. You find greater pleasure when you can have both—perhaps a "quickie" followed by sustained passionate physical interaction. You like to dictate the timing and circumstances. You like to penetrate your partner's defenses, teasing him or her into a state of intense physical excitement. Remember, force is not the only way, or even the best way, to accomplish your goal. Try humor as a sexual tool.

Sun in Taurus (fixed earth)

You bring your soul to physical passion. You also bring humor with you, and can occasionally find yourself laughing out loud when sex goes either well or badly. You love the pleasure given and received through sex. You can be jealous of your partner, sexually and in every other way as well. This emotion can dampen physical passion. You will want to work through jealous feelings on the logical level so you can set them aside. You can be selfish, which can work for you in terms of physical pleasure: the more pleasure you give to your partner, the more you are likely to receive.

Sun in Gemini (mutable air)

You sometimes worry about your ability to satisfy your partner, yet you are versatile and willing to try anything. Use your hands—they express your feelings effectively, and they can tantalize your partner. You love life and view sex as a natural part of life. When you find the right partner, you are willing to study his or her desires and needs until you know just what to do each time you are together. You personally love change. Discover what your partner wants—too much experimentation could be a bad thing. You like a balance of power and a very light touch.

Sun in Cancer (cardinal water)

You get the most pleasure when you enter a sexual experience through the proper emotional doorway. While you like high drama, you don't especially enjoy risky situations. Sex is best for you when you feel protected. A familiar environment and a sympathetic partner are requirements. Then you can add imagination to heighten your excitement. You love to make love; plain sex is not as compelling. Ask your partner to help create a harmonious atmosphere in which you can appreciate his or her attention and flattery. Sex may be best late at night.

Sun in Leo (fixed fire)

You like to lord it over others, but where sex is concerned, you seek approval. Your sensuality includes physical touch, emotional stimulation, mental encouragement, and spiritual heightening of passion. You enjoy the dominant position and can be demanding where sex is concerned. You find that long-term relationships are more likely to provide the intensity you seek. You have a cruel edge sometimes, which will probably not enhance your sex life. You can be a bit selfish. You have to let your partner know what you want; then devote yourself to discovering what your partner desires.

Sun in Virgo (mutable earth)

There is method in your sex life. You are meticulous about the setting as well as the players. Because you tend to judge your success by the results, you pay close attention to your partner's responses as well as your own satisfaction. You sometimes are overly critical of your own performance. You are not one to jump into the middle of the sexual process. Foreplay, for you, starts when you get dressed for dinner, or maybe even when you make the date. You tend to maintain mental reserve. To overcome this, you must feel secure with your partner. Satisfaction and contentment depend on honesty in your sexual relationship.

Sun in Libra (cardinal air)

On the surface, sexuality is all about beauty, art, and refinement. You set exacting standards in appearance and demeanor. You are a romantic—sometimes you find the sweaty details of sex a bit off-putting. By the same token, you very much appreciate the partner who takes all that into account, adapts to your sensibilities, and still delivers the full impact of a great physical experience. Your best sexual experiences are those that integrate physical touch with emotional impact. Your fires are embedded deeply in your personality and demand a partner who is willing to draw them to the surface.

Sun in Scorpio (fixed water)

Scorpio seeks attachment. Bold, even aggressive sex can be seen as one way to ensure attachment. Scorpio can also turn on the magnetism like no other sign, drawing a sexual partner into a creative, healing physical encounter. How to avoid dominating and controlling your partner? That is Scorpio's question. The solution is taking the time to develop trust, having the courage to express your needs and desires, and having the determination to fulfill your partner, even when that means going to sexual places that don't particularly attract you. And remember, excess seems fun at the time, but can be quite painful later.

Sun in Sagittarius (mutable fire)

You are idealistic about life and love. Your athletic skills play a big part in achieving sexual prowess. However, the goal is superb ecstasy, not athletic achievement. Let's talk about surrendering to your passion. Here I want to mention exercising restraint. You don't have to rush your partner to orgasm. Take your time, be open to alternative methods, and expand your understanding of erogenous zones. Your partner could turn out to have sensitive areas you never read about in books. Indulge your partner's whims, but don't buy into anything so extreme that it causes fear or a loss of trust.

Sun in Capricorn (cardinal earth)

You're really pretty conservative, so sex for you can be traditional and therefore somewhat boring. Instead of looking around for a new partner, try keeping your current sexual partner satisfied by adding new techniques, expanding your sense of romance, or engaging in slightly dark, secretive, erotic efforts. Chocolate in all its forms comes to mind as a part of foreplay. Dark wines and a variety of flavors in tasty morsels can stimulate the senses. Touching the skin with ice may send you right over the top (but could be a major turnoff for your partner). You believe to your core in responsible sex.

Sun in Aquarius (fixed air)

You have superior powers of observation. This may not seem like a skill to use in your sex life, but think about it. You can catalog each encounter, log the successes, and rank them in some order. You have a storehouse of information about human nature that can be applied in each unique sexual encounter. You rebel against the norm, and therefore are likely to consider—and try—a wide variety of sexual activities. Through cooperation you and your partner are able to reach greater heights of physical pleasure.

Sun in Pisces (mutable water)

Your spiritual side has probably considered renouncing the world and its physical pleasures, but you may want to rethink that position. You become devoted to your sexual partner quickly. Hint: if you don't realistically see a future in a relationship, don't have sex, as you could be bitterly disappointed. To find the best partner, let intuition be your guide. You are generally modest, which could limit your choices if you think you are not worthy. Actually, you offer tremendous gifts of emotional responsiveness and romantic inclination, along with adaptability to many sexual styles.

The Sun Through the Houses

The house position of your Sun reveals an especially important area of your life. Consider the role sex plays in each area of your life, and how you can best satisfy your sexual needs. You will quickly see that some areas of life are more conducive to sex than others.

Sun in the First House

You want to be in control of your life. Controlling sex actually means controlling the method and moment when you lose control. Remember surrender? Surrender is a good thing only when you have cultivated your passion, focused your consciousness on your goal of physical fulfillment, and secured a partnership in which you can express your passionate emotions boldly. Your spirit aligns with your persona perfectly when sexual passion strikes the right chord.

Sun in the Second House

You identify closely with your own actions, and your self-esteem suffers when you do anything that is outside your ethical code. This means you must avoid any sexual encounter that doesn't feel appropriate. Don't be rushed into sex with a near stranger. Instead, demand that the relationship grow for both of you, and allow intimacy to increase gradually. Don't get me wrong—you benefit from physical fulfillment as much as anyone, but it has to be comfortable on every level to achieve the best results.

Sun in the Third House

Versatility is your middle name. When one sexual technique or approach doesn't work, you try another. And another. You are willing to learn something new from your sexual partner(s), and you may experiment with multiple partners or with more than one relationship at a time. Your sexual libido fluctuates, depending largely on the information you absorb from your environment. Thus the setting has a huge impact on your sexual performance and enjoyment.

Sun in the Fourth House

You like to have sex at home because you like the secure, familiar surroundings. You know exactly where the shower is and where to find the dish for your dessert. You also love the idea of bringing your lover to your place, where you have arranged everything perfectly. You hate tripping over someone else's furniture in the dark. A strong, lasting relationship is a deep source of joy that you should not jeopardize for the sake of a one-night stand. Once in the sexual moment, you flow into passion, achieving a Niagara Falls level of ecstasy.

Sun in the Fifth House

While sex is not a game for you, it certainly is fun. You love the creative dynamic that can be felt only with intense intimacy. Therefore you take extra time and care to prepare the sexual environment and make it feel safe before you even begin. For this game to be played well, you believe, the surroundings must support both partners. You have one eye on the future too. The best games, after all, require the development of skill. You want a partner who knows your deepest desires and has the skill and staying power to deliver.

Sun in the Sixth House

You can be a bit clinical about sex. You want the setting to be fresh and clean—even sanitary. You want all the essentials close at hand. You take a somewhat orderly approach to sex, at least when making the arrangements. However, once you are in the midst of sexual passion, you want a partner who pays attention to your needs and desires, just as you pay attention to his or hers. You tend to notice any problems, which can interfere with the pleasure of sex.

Sun in the Seventh House

You require partnership in your life. The sexual component of partnership can take you to a new level of understanding of life and love if you let it. What's required? Commitment is the first and foremost factor. Your partner must be as loyal as you are. Cooperative effort enhances sexual pleasure for both of you—cooperation is far more important than experience or even skill. You like a decisive partner, but don't want to be forced in any way.

Sun in the Eighth House

You have erotic dreams that pique your sexual interest. They provide a doorway from ordinary experience to the world beyond the daily grind, and you seek to open that doorway consciously through sexual activity. Massage is a good adjunct to sexual pleasure, as muscular tension detracts from your enjoyment. You focus on the external sex organs. Actual intercourse may not be as exciting as foreplay for this reason. You need to negotiate with your partner to make sure you both fulfill each other's sexual desires.

Sun in the Ninth House

Being a restless, mobile person, your sexual pleasure is enhanced by substantial movement. You are willing to experiment with novel, even athletic, sexual positions. You relish change and can benefit from shifting positions several times during a single sexual engagement. An alternative is to remain virtually still while your partner moves. You enjoy talk that allows your mind to race. This could include words about philosophically high-minded topics. It could also include statements about what your partner is about to do.

Sun in the Tenth House

Your natural ability to focus can be a huge sexual asset. Concentration on the intimate task at hand is much appreciated. You want to be assured that your partner is present and attentive at all times. Fewer distractions are better for your sex life. Tireless effort is appreciated too. You thrive in public environments, but this is not the best place for sexual intimacy. However, if your partner whispers appropriate sweet nothings in your ear at parties, that will surely get you out the door and on the way to your own bedroom.

Sun in the Eleventh House

You are not satisfied with the missionary position. You want to experiment with different positions, styles, and environmental stimuli in order to experience the richness of sexual possibilities. You are generally willing to work with your partner in these experiments. If your attitude comes across as overly aloof, or if you appear to desire extreme sex to the detriment of "good" sex, you may find your partner less than enthusiastic. Physically you need strong (not painful) stimulation to keep you in the physical realm.

Sun in the Twelfth House

You like your sex to be comfortable. You like a slow, even dreamy approach, with plenty of foreplay to get you in the mood. Disturbing music, television in the background, or crying children can interrupt your mood and leave you almost incapable of achieving physical satisfaction. This being the case, you need to set the mood for sexual intimacy and ensure as few interruptions as possible. Then engage your psychic awareness to enhance both your partner's experience and your own.

Sun Aspects

The Sun's aspects indicate the channels through which sexual stimulation works best for you. In chapter 15 you can read about the Sun's aspects in your chart. Consider how (or if) these interpretations match up with your recent sexual experiences. You can heighten your sensitivity and response by accommodating your own needs, as reflected by the aspects.

4
Mercury
The Mental Side

Yes, there is a mental side to sex. We actually spend a considerable amount of time thinking sexual thoughts. We are intelligent, thinking beings. We thrive in situations where we can apply our critical thinking to problems. This means that our thoughts, while often tending toward where and how to get sex, also focus on ways to improve our sex lives.

Even in the arenas of romance and sexuality, thinking through your feelings can be helpful. Sometimes you have to delay gratification. The delay actually can improve the outcome when you finally come together with your partner. Fools rush in. Sexual fools rush through the sexual experience, and miss out on heightened feelings of prolonged sexual contact. On the other hand, sometimes rushing is exactly what's called for!

Your approach to thinking about sexuality may be different from that of your partner, and it's good to understand those differences. Each of you has ideas and beliefs that play a part in how you approach sex. Understanding your different beliefs moves your sexual relationship to a higher level. At first you just know that you want the other person. As the relationship grows, you pay more attention to subtle cues from your partner. Both of you are then able to provide more profound satisfaction for each other.

The following descriptions of Mercury in each sign reveal twelve rather different approaches to the mental side of sex. Read about your own sign, but also read the others, and think about the differences. After all, differences can add a certain spice to your sex life.

Mercury in the Signs

Mercury in Aries

You are a creative thinker. Where sex is concerned, you can always think of a new position, new scenario, or new attitude to bring to the encounter. You like to talk about it too. In your enthusiasm you may tell your partner how he or she can improve performance, creating a sense of inferiority or incompetence rather than pleasure. When this happens, you know it right away and try to make up for the slip of the tongue with renewed effort. You benefit from writing down your thoughts afterward for future reference. This frees you to enjoy the moment as it happens.

Mercury in Taurus

You are adept at formal thinking and logic. You understand the practical application of logic and take a deliberate approach to most activities. You tend to be somewhat one-sided in your thinking. Where sexuality is concerned, you benefit both from thinking through what you really want, and from opening your mind to new possibilities. This doesn't mean you have to try everything you hear or read about. It does mean that communication with your partner can expand the range of sexual pleasure in your relationship.

Mercury in Gemini

You are quite flexible in your thinking. Your sex life has all the variety imaginable, but may lack the comfort and satisfaction that can come from consistency and a steady effort. You love change, and your partner can become exhausted just thinking about so many sexual possibilities. It's likely that your verbal skills will get you into and out of all sorts of sexual jams with your steady partner and/or one-night stands. In other words, your mouth is not your best weapon in the Battle of the Sexes. Let your imagination run wild, but keep most of your thoughts to yourself.

Mercury in Cancer

Your perceptions are a combination of thinking and feeling. Where sexuality is concerned, you are able to immerse yourself deeply in the physical feelings and emotions surrounding intimacy. You are not afraid to try something new that pops into your head, and you are willing to pay attention to feedback from your partner. There is a subtle, relentless quality to your lovemaking, like water flowing downhill—you will pursue sexual satisfaction until you experience it. When you are not in the mood for sex, forget it. Your mind is elsewhere.

Mercury in Leo

You bring joyful enthusiasm to your sex life. If Tigger could harness his exuberance, he would be a mirror image of your passion for passion. You want your sex life planned out—your enthusiasm has little to do with surprises. You sometimes treat your sexual partner as a possession. This may work for a while, but others tire of your constant management. Overall results are better when you let your sexual partner handle the planning and execution some of the time. A word of advice: don't take risks in the sex department. Loyalty is a powerful ally.

Mercury in Virgo

You want to know everything. Sex is no different from any other arena—you consider every detail. This means that you explore your partner's body and know it as well as your own. You think about what you discover and apply it to lovemaking. Eventually you become something of an expert at setting the stage, gathering the appropriate costumes, and playing out the sexual scene. It's your attention to detail that makes you a successful sexual partner. Or is it the fact that you think of sex as a partnership activity?

Mercury in Libra

Teamwork is definitely part of your sex life. You put a lot of creative thought into how the two of you can become more excited, more satisfied, more fulfilled. You are willing to try some edgy stuff, but always within a balanced and respectful framework. Most of the time, your good manners are part of the sexual pattern. Occasionally, though, you have to surrender fully to passion and give up any pretense of decorum. The more beautiful the ambiance, the more you enjoy sex. Maybe it shouldn't matter, but it does, so create a setting that works for you.

Mercury in Scorpio

Some of your best career skills are really not that helpful in sexual activities. For example, skepticism is good beforehand, but during the act you have to make an all-out commitment. Criticism has no place in the bedroom either. Now, endurance is another matter. You may be able to outlast the Energizer Bunny in bed. Finding solutions—this is another skill your partner will appreciate when a problem arises. Transform your thinking, and you will improve your sex life. Transform your partner's thinking, and you will revolutionize your sex life.

Mercury in Sagittarius

You are a thinker. Where sex is concerned, this can be a definite advantage, as you think about each sexual encounter beforehand. You bring all your intellectual and intuitive forces to bear on the question of how to get the most out of your sex life. Of course, you can overdo the thinking process, and then sex is ungrounded and even somewhat without feeling. You have a storytelling ability that could be a source of fun where sex is concerned. For example, you could create an image in your partner's mind of sexy scenarios that are missing from your immediate environment.

Mercury in Capricorn

You are thorough and patient. You are willing to work at your sex life in order to achieve the highest and best fulfillment. Casual sex, for you, is not worth having. If your ambitions turn toward sex, you could make a career out of being the most sought-after partner. Or you could earn your living through sex-related products. You can always enact scenes in which you are paying or being paid for sex, just to add some spice.

Mercury in Aquarius

Your progressive thinking leads you to try new things. In the sexual arena this brings variety into the picture, and variety is the spice of life. You are an enthusiastic sex partner, and you can be quite inventive. Try to remember your partner's preferences and incorporate them frequently. New is not always better. Instead, build upon what is already working well. Revisit an established technique, and perfect it. You are willing to enjoy sex alone. As you explore your own sexual desires, you improve your performance with a partner.

Mercury in Pisces

Your mind is like a sponge, soaking up the thoughts and feelings of others very easily. Your sex life is enhanced when you are open to your partner's desires. You can create the ultimate fantasy setting for sexual encounters, and the variety of your imagination is virtually boundless. The downside is that you can get lost in your imagination and lose the physical connection that is necessary for sexual fulfillment. When floating on the sea of sensuality, you can anchor yourself through your senses of taste and smell.

Mercury Through the Houses

Mercury in the First House

Sometimes, it seems like sex really is all about you and very little about your partner. This can be especially true when you speak carelessly. Observe your partner's response as well as your own. Then use your creative mind to improve mutual satisfaction exponentially.

Mercury in the Second House

You are patient. If your partner is not on the same wavelength all the time, you are willing to wait or to work on changing the wavelength. You won't wait forever, but you are flexible. Don't wear out your vocal cords talking about the mundane details of your sex life. Deliberate actions speak louder than casual words.

Mercury in the Third House

You love variety and seek out new experiences. If your partner is too humdrum, you are tempted to stray. An overly casual approach sends the message that you don't really care beyond the physical act itself. In paying attention to the details, your planning for sexual encounters will have fantastic results.

Mercury in the Fourth House

Regardless of your thinking style, you are usually able to establish a close connection between thoughts and feelings. Once involved in a sexual encounter, you immerse yourself in the experience and shut out distractions easily. You develop your own set of sexual "tools" that make your partner's experience that much more powerful.

Mercury in the Fifth House

Your creative mind is always developing a plan for the next sexual encounter. You leave little to chance where sex is concerned. Your enthusiasm draws your partner into greater enjoyment and physical passion. With an eye on the future, you want your partner to be around for a long time.

Mercury in the Sixth House

You like to think of yourself as an expert in the sex department. You need to acquire some experience before you can think of yourself as a sexual virtuoso. You tend to focus on the details and forget the larger picture, but you are a master at eliciting your partner's cooperation and enthusiasm for sex.

Mercury in the Seventh House

You appreciate good manners. In your sex life this means clean body, clean hands, orderly environment, and even a ritual approach to each other. Preparing the space for sex is different from preparing it for sleep. Light candles, dim the lights, and add a touch of natural perfume to set the sexual mood.

Mercury in the Eighth House

You can be sharply critical. This will shut down your partner's sexual response like nothing else. There is no place for sarcasm where physical pleasure is concerned. You are better off discussing your preferences ahead of time and listening to your partner's desires. Then you can enjoy sexuality without argument or back talk.

Mercury in the Ninth House

Part of your mind always seems to be in the future, which is not the ideal place to experience powerful sexual satisfaction. You are fully capable of planning the most romantic, exotic sexual encounters. When the moment comes, let go of your mental expectations, and pay attention to the physical experience.

Mercury in the Tenth House

Your sex life becomes more satisfying through your own efforts rather than those of your partner. The more conscious you are of your own physical desires, the better experience you can have. Don't just let your partner do whatever—talk about the nuts and bolts of sexual satisfaction. Or show your partner what you want!

Mercury in the Eleventh House

Inventive sex is on your mind a lot. You imagine all sorts of possibilities. Reading the *Kama Sutra* may give you ideas about ancient sexual techniques. The main thing, though, is that you view each sexual excursion as a unique event to be savored and enjoyed. You are quick to understand your partner's mood.

Mercury in the Twelfth House

Your partner's requests draw you away from your own desires. If your partner reciprocates, all is well. If not, you have to make your own desires known. Because you have an active fantasy life, you may be the source of the most unusual and dramatic sexual adventures in your partnership.

Mercury Aspects

Aspects between Mercury and the other planets reveal profound subtleties where your sex life is concerned. You have your own basic way of thinking about sex, and then you have additional ideas that modify that view. From time to time, as the planets move into and out of aspect, you find that your sexual thinking takes a very different direction. Refer to chapter 15 for information about each of your Mercury aspects.

5
The Moon
Emotional Needs

We are all aware that emotions play a huge role in sexuality. If you have ever been unable to engage in sex because of your emotions, you know this. By understanding the emotional differences between you and your partner, you take a giant step toward greater physical satisfaction.

Noel Tyl, Jeffrey Green, and other astrologers have talked about the Moon in terms of the reigning need of the personality.[1] This need is so profound that an individual will sometimes pursue it without regard to the impact on the self and others—the less conscious need can be so powerful that efforts to fulfill it sometimes make no logical sense. To illustrate an extreme case of need, suppose you are starving. You will eat whatever is available. You will disregard religious precepts, steal, or even kill to obtain food. After all, if you starve to death, nothing else matters anyway.

Yet we have examples of people who have foregone food for some reason. A mother may feed her children before herself because her need to save them is more important than her own hunger. Religious figures have endured hunger strikes to make an ethical or moral point. Closer to home, sometimes you are so engrossed in what you are doing that you ignore hunger signals for hours. We can conclude that no human need is absolute.

The Moon in your chart is a good indicator of your reigning need. It is also a good barometer of your sexual needs. The Moon reflects all of your emotional responses. Even if your Moon indicates needs that have very little to do with sexuality, within your emotional package is a need associated with physical pleasure. Because there are twelve signs, there are at the very least twelve distinct ways people approach sexual needs. The interpretations that follow focus on how your emotional needs are likely to express themselves in terms of sexuality. The more you understand your own basic needs and those of your partner, the better you will be able to create appropriate environments in which to enjoy sexuality.

The Moon in the Signs

Moon in Aries

You have two powerful emotional needs: the need to take action and the need for power. When these needs are in charge, you are probably too forceful to be an attractive sexual companion because you demand all the attention and control. When you control the need to act, you are able to build to a more powerful climax in any activity, not the least of which is sex. When you control the need for power, you develop the capacity to surrender to the sheer pleasure of physical stimulation. And sometimes you get to be on top.

Moon in Taurus

Your need for comfort helps you create a private, secure environment for most sexual activities. Your need for pleasure is a natural stimulus for a sexual relationship. Your need for enjoyment can be channeled into a matrix in which you pay attention to your partner's needs as much as your own. After all, your enjoyment is enhanced when your partner is having a great sexual experience too. When allowed to run rampant, these needs manifest as excess and can jeopardize your material security.

Moon in Gemini

For you, self-expression is a paramount need. This can be a powerful sexual driver, as sex is certainly one way to express your need for companionship and connection. Sometimes you continue to express your opinion well after you have made an essential point, which can be a major turnoff. At other times, your needs seem superficial and even silly to other people. What they may not realize is that underneath that thin façade, you have profound depths. Your light verbal approach is a reflection of your effort to reduce the degree of change in your life.

Moon in Cancer

You are naturally affectionate. Your best sexual fulfillment comes after you have satisfied other sides of your nature. They say the way to a person's heart is through the stomach, and this is definitely true for you. When you are hungry, you are distracted from sexual matters. Eat first, and have sex later.

You need to arrange every facet of a romantic encounter to maximize sexual pleasure. This is because you sometimes have a hard time shutting out thoughts and impressions and focusing on the moment. You are likely to keep your love nest in a state of general readiness at all times. Remember, scents are powerful sexual stimulants. Use your favorites wisely.

Moon in Leo

You are naturally intuitive, and you seek to connect at that level. You are creative, and you need to constantly experience the creative mode. You also desire to be noticed and will go to some lengths to get attention, even when your efforts are not constructive. Paradoxically, to fulfill your reigning needs, you need to rein in your drives. Allow intuition to flow instead of pushing for that all-important connection. Develop a variety of creative skills so you don't run out of fun projects. Finally, as you develop strong interpersonal connections and materially manifest your creative talent, you naturally receive the attention you seek.

Moon in Virgo

You need to understand the intimate details of sex. Even in the midst of a passionate moment, you are considering the practical aspects of the situation. Your approach to sex is somewhat methodical, and you love a tidy environment. Take care of the neatness details ahead of time, and have everything you will want or need available. Then allow yourself to explore new ways to pleasure your partner—and yourself. Hint: learn to relax your mind and enjoy the details of physical sensation. For you, sex without love and respect is a pale imitation of the real thing.

Moon in Libra

Your dominant needs often run counter to each other. On the one hand, you need love and affection. You will go to great lengths to receive affection, including capitulating to your partner's desires. When you do, you sometimes feel cheated or shortchanged. On the other hand, you need to indulge yourself. Where sex is concerned, this can mean enthusiastic engagement in whatever sexual activity enters your mind. It can get out of hand very easily, leaving both you and your partner disappointed or even angry. Balance is the key to satisfying both needs.

Moon in Scorpio

You think your main drive is to achieve physical satisfaction, but when you are done with that phase of sexual intimacy, you are sometimes left wishing for more. This is due to your underlying need for emotional stimulation. A lot of the time you guard your feelings so closely that you can't or won't go to a deeper level with sex. You also have a deep survival instinct that prevents you from taking the risk involved with total surrender to sexual passion. Even though you continue to hesitate at the brink of surrender, with experience you will find that giving in is well worth the risk.

Moon in Sagittarius

Your need for change and variety in your life can lead to a series of semisatisfactory relationships in which sex never reaches the maximum high. You never stay in one relationship long enough to get to profound levels of sensation and emotion that are the essence of sexual pleasure. You also want action in your life. If you can connect with a partner who is willing to travel or let you travel, that will satisfy your desire for action. Then you can continue to develop depth of intimacy within one relationship.

Moon in Capricorn

Your driving need for career success can be channeled into a desire for sexual success. Sexual satisfaction and ecstasy constitute a two-way street along which you and your partner travel. There is an uphill slope that leads to the heights of physical pleasure. It takes two to get up that hill. Your second need is to insulate your feelings. This one can really prevent you from having the best sexual experience. One way to work with this need is to establish a home that insulates you from the outer world. There your sex life has a place to bloom and grow, and you can pour out your feelings in safety.

Moon in Aquarius

Independence is the central guiding factor in your decision-making process. You rarely choose to do anything that you perceive will limit your activities. When you get into the occasional restrictive situation, you don't walk away—you run! The need for change is thus satisfied, but at what cost? The best partner for you is the one who can make you believe that all decisions are your choice and that all ideas originate with you. There aren't many partners around who meet this qualification. You enjoy sex more when you find ways to feel independent outside your relationship and to develop your cooperative strengths within your partnership.

Moon in Pisces

Your reigning need is for sympathy. Interestingly, you also need to demonstrate sympathy for others. Early in your sexual life you may not manage these needs very well, which will limit the level of pleasure you can achieve. When you both give and receive sympathetic understanding in the present moment, then your sex life begins to move up the scale of satisfaction. Your second need is to yield to your partner. Again, though, your partner expects you to pursue so he or she can yield on occasion. Explore the range of your personal needs so you understand how they function in your life. Then movement along the continuum from selfish to selfless is possible.

The Moon Through the Houses

Whereas the Moon sign indicates the most powerful needs within the personality, the house placement of the Moon suggests the arena in which those needs can best be satisfied. Thus each Moon sign finds sexual satisfaction in twelve different ways, depending on the house placement of the Moon in the birth chart.

Moon in the First House

Your basic needs can best be satisfied in activities that involve physical touch. Your head may be particularly sensitive to physical touch. So while the sex act is very important, you also enjoy whispers in the ear, a light hand smoothing your face, and the feel of your lover brushing your hair.

Moon in the Second House

When seeking to satisfy your basic needs, look to the physical comfort of your surroundings. You relish different colors and textures of fabric, a scent to set the mood, and even a variety of foods to stimulate your taste buds. A rich variety of satisfactions enhances the sexual experience for you.

Moon in the Third House

You have great sex in environments that are too busy for your partner. You can be talking, petting, or listening to music, and still stay focused on the sexual matters at hand. Your partner may have a tougher time maintaining intimate contact when all that is going on. Keep this strong difference of attitude and approach in mind when you plan your next intimate date.

Moon in the Fourth House

Face it, sex at home is best for you. Hotel rooms just don't have the right ambiance. In fact, sex with your reliable, long-time partner will satisfy your needs more deeply than occasional sex ever could. Devise sexual signals that only you and your partner understand. That way you can escape a party and get back home to your carefully decorated love nest.

Moon in the Fifth House

Children are significant in your life, but they are not the only reason to have sex. Your creativity can grow in other directions with the right sexual partner. You and your partner can develop an intuitive awareness of each other that enhances sexual pleasure. Don't skimp where sex is concerned. An elegant setting and enticing attire add spice to your sex life.

Moon in the Sixth House

Your sex life is as much about satisfying your partner as it is about being satisfied. To achieve the highest satisfaction, go beyond mere service. Employ your practical skills to satisfy your subconscious fantasies. Discover your partner's fantasies too. No detail is too small, but let go of the details once you are in the intimate moment.

Moon in the Seventh House

Without a long-term partner, you can achieve physical satisfaction but fail to reach your full potential for spiritual bliss. Fate is a factor in your partnership. You may meet your partner when you are not looking or expecting to find love. Once found, you have to take steps to make the relationship grow. You have to get off the fence in order to pursue your sexual passion.

Moon in the Eighth House

Your sex life can feel like a long series of struggles. You reach the greatest contentment when sexuality includes a spiritual component. You and your partner are able to satisfy each other's physical desires from the beginning. You grow into a deeper relationship through struggles for survival, and these efforts are reflected in a profound spiritual connection. The deeper the spiritual connection, the hotter the sexual flame burns.

Moon in the Ninth House

Your inner life is vivid and dramatic. You alternate between states of pessimism and optimism, and the state you are in has a major effect on your sexual experience. Remember that everything changes, including your mood. The right setting can quickly bring you to a sexually alert status, even if you were sure a few minutes earlier that sex was the furthest thing from your mind.

Moon in the Tenth House

Sex is not a responsibility—it's a potential career. No, you aren't destined to become a prostitute. Still, when you bring the same professional attitude to your sex life that you invest in your career, you find that sex provides a much broader field for personal expression. The investment of time and effort will be worth it.

Moon in the Eleventh House

You need to be involved in group or community activities. However, you will find that most people think of sex as a private, two-person affair. You thrive in situations that demand clear thinking. Sexual intimacy is not a mindless activity. It requires focused attention on yourself, your partner, and the matter at hand. Focus your imagination on the moment, and you can't go wrong.

Moon in the Twelfth House

Two things are essential for your sexual pleasure: privacy and more privacy. You are not one to put your sex life on display. Oh, you may dress for passion, but when the moment comes, it had better be in a safe, secure, private environment. Then you can really let your hair down. Not one to kiss and tell, you expect the same from your partner.

Moon Aspects

The Moon's aspects indicate ways for you to enhance your emotional pleasure. If you have any sexual experience at all, you know that some things work in one situation and flop miserably in another. The connections between your Moon and the rest of your chart indicate the most direct ways for you to satisfy your sexual desires. They also indicate the challenges you face in achieving peak sexual experiences. You can explore your lunar aspects in chapter 15.

---

1. Noel Tyl, *Synthesis & Counseling in Astrology* (St. Paul, MN: Llewellyn Publications, 1998) p. 2.

6
Neptune
Spiritual Ecstasy Through Physical Relationships

Spirituality has a different meaning for each of us. The multiplicity of religions through-out the world shows us that the human spirit searches for meaning in many different places and faces. Gods and goddesses abound. Even aboriginal animism reflects the very human need to understand the world around us, and to make sense of it through spirits that inhabit everything.

While scientists are busy attempting to define every facet of our lives empirically, we are each busy creating, sustaining, and destroying our own spiritual beliefs in an effort to find the perfect credos by which to guide our lives. Sexuality, being an important part of our lives, is open to spiritual influence. Sexual impulses can lift us beyond our ordinary lives to a spiritual level of consciousness.

People take many avenues to enhance both spiritual and sexual experience. Some religions include tantric or similar practices that are designed to elevate consciousness through sexual drives. Kundalini yoga focuses on the energy that rises from the root chakra and stimulates the sexual power center in the body on its way to other chakras and higher consciousness centers. The drug culture both exalts sexual experience and preys on people through sex. Generally you will find that drugs alter your immediate sexual experience, but you find little lasting satisfaction from sex and drugs. Tantra and yoga, in contrast, heighten your ability to focus on physical sensation and stimulate a higher spiritual connection with your partner, thereby enhancing the sexual experience.

Two planets, Mars and Neptune, provide indications of passion, compassion, and devotion in our charts. They indicate two very different views of these functions. This chapter will consider passion and devotion from the Neptunian perspective; Mars will be discussed with Venus in a later chapter on individual motivations.

Generally speaking, as you cultivate any relationship, you achieve a deeper connection to your partner. In sexually motivated relationships, longer-term relationships lead to higher and higher levels of physical satisfaction. In addition, your spiritual connection is developing. Knowing each other spiritually enhances physical satisfaction immeasurably. The constructive side of Neptune leads to wisdom that goes beyond logical, rational thought. Neptune's energy often includes clairvoyance and other psychic faculties. It is a factor in artistic expression of all kinds. The entertaining side of Neptune includes glamour that covers up the truth; films, acting, and otherwise portraying a story that is not your own; imaginative storytelling; and a host of other creative activities. The less constructive side of Neptune includes deceit, self-indulgence, and chaotic thoughts and emotions. Neptune's energy has a broad range of expression, from sublime heights to slimy depths.

The Neptune key to sexual expression actually involves all levels of human experience. Deceit can ruin a relationship, but a surprise or a bit of glamour can stimulate and enhance sexual interest. By the same token, if your attention is totally focused on transcendent thoughts, you won't fully appreciate the physical side of your sex life.

Neptune moves very slowly through the signs, which means that everyone in your general age group probably has Neptune in the same sign. (Note that the dates for the signs overlap because of Neptune's apparent movement backward—*retrograde* motion—through the zodiac.) Neptune's house placement and aspects are more significant than its sign. The house placement shows the area of your life in which this planet is most prominent. The aspects show how Neptune's energy tends to work itself out in your life.

Neptune in the Signs

Because it moves so slowly, no one alive today has Neptune in Pisces, Aries, Taurus, or Gemini, and few people have it in Leo.

Neptune in Aries

About 1861–1874; 2025–2039.

You have a natural love of humanity. Your emotions run the entire range of feelings. You are sometimes confused about your objectives where sexuality is concerned.

Neptune in Taurus

1874–1889; 2038–2052.

You tend to be moody, so your sex life is likely to run in cycles too. Overuse of drugs can dull your sexual appetite or your degree of physical satisfaction from sex.

Neptune in Gemini

1887–1902; 2051–2066.

You tend toward mystical thinking and may lack practical focus. When your sexual fantasies are satisfied, your physical satisfaction increases exponentially.

Neptune in Cancer

1901–1915; 2065–2079.

You have an affectionate nature and thrive in a sexual relationship that emphasizes love. You can become depressed or unstable without sex or some other way for you to connect to the material world. Sex can accomplish that for you in part.

Neptune in Leo

1914–1929; 2078–2093.

Generally enthusiastic, you have lots of plans. You occasionally experience periods of little forward progress. Your sex life can reflect the cycle of optimism and pessimism.

Neptune in Virgo

1928–1943; 2092–2107.

You connect with your partner through your psychic senses. Sex can be wildly exciting when the psychic link goes both ways. Sex may improve with age because you have learned more about your own sensitivity and seek out situations that feel right to you. In addition, you tend to be less critical as you gain general life experience, and this adaptability is a plus in the sexual arena.

Neptune in Libra

1942–1957; 2105–2120.

You are receptive to ideas from other people and to sexual overtures as well. In youth, you are less realistic and may find that your sex life suffers when you make poor choices. With age and experience, you learn to see potential sexual partners with two sets of eyes—one focused on the magnetism between you, and the other on practical realities.

Neptune in Scorpio

1955–1970; 2119–2134.

Your senses tune in to subtle messages from your sexual partner. At the same time, you are also receiving messages from within yourself. When you merge with your partner, you sometimes get rushes of psychic information. The metaphysical realm becomes congruent with the physical realm. Because of this strong affinity, all sexual encounters deserve conscious thought and careful choice. Be sure you want those psychic vibes from a potential partner before you get into bed.

Neptune in Sagittarius

1970–1984; 2133–2148.

You are often able to foresee outcomes. Applied to your sex life, this skill has a deepening effect. You make fewer errors in judgment as you get to know your partner better. Use your intuition, and then ask your partner—it's always good to confirm a fantasy before you get too deep into playing it out. Now here's the tricky part: you need to examine your partner's fantasies the same way. This requires an excellent level of verbal communication between you.

Neptune in Capricorn

1984–1998; 2148–2162.

One of your greatest strengths in the sexual arena is your capacity to explore every possibility deeply and thoroughly. You believe that if something is worth trying, it is worth exploring. Thus you are not put off by an initial failure. You are willing to modify your technique through experimentation. Allow your partner to provide a strong dose of reality from time to time, and your sex life will stay on track.

Neptune in Aquarius

1998–2012; 2161–2176.

You seek a soul mate with whom to share sex and everything else in your life. You have unique powers of attraction that draw potential partners to you. You have to learn to sort through the possibilities without the necessity of jumping into bed with everyone who comes along. To attract your soul mate, you must maintain your physical appearance, mental flexibility, emotional loyalty, and spiritual awareness. Yes, you can handle all that.

Neptune in Pisces

2011–2036; 2175–2190.

You can sink into weird, even pathological sexuality, or you can insulate yourself with a degree of reserve that keeps everyone away from you. Between these extremes, you can develop profound mystical talent. Your psychic senses can light up a physical relationship, revealing your partner's hidden needs and desires. Controlling the impulse to indulge in drugs is essential for sexual fulfillment.

Neptune Through the Houses

Neptune in the First House

Your nervous system is sensitive to the lightest physical or psychic touch. Knowing this, be sure you choose sexual partners who are aware of your needs and desires, and not just caught up in personal desire. When you share a psychic connection with your partner, the physical component of sex is immeasurably enhanced for both of you. Deeper sexual pleasure generates emotional responses you don't usually associate with physical satisfaction. For example, you can experience sadness right along with immense joy.

Neptune in the Second House

Your moods completely dictate your sex life. Whether male or female, you find yourself saying, "Not now—I have a headache," to cover other feelings you can't even explain to yourself. Your physical stamina fluctuates along with your moods. You would be wise to avoid drugs whenever possible. Walking meditation can boost your mental concentration and can have a positive impact on your physical endurance as well.

Neptune in the Third House

Because you are impressionable, you absorb energy from your sexual partner. It's imperative that the two of you have open communication to avoid misunderstandings about the source or direction of each other's emotions. It's possible they are not directed toward you at all. Your mystical tendencies can become a significant facet of your sex life when you cultivate shared ecstatic experiences of all kinds, sex included.

Neptune in the Fourth House

Your core beliefs emerge into consciousness through psychic sensitivity. Your capacity to feel the union between you and your partner depends on these closely held beliefs, so it's very helpful to understand what is truly important to you on the spiritual level. Your deep sensitivity can lead to disappointment in your sex life, but it is also a resource to enhance your pleasure. Water or body oils enhance your sexual response, so jump in the bath together!

Neptune in the Fifth House

Sexual enthusiasm spreads to spiritual creativity. You see your sex life as an integral part of your spiritual life. Any sexual activity that falls below your set standards should be avoided. Carelessness allows you to misdirect your passion into side ventures that have little meaning. Therefore you need to focus on your sexual partnership, avoid excessive drama, and engage in seductive activities only with appropriate partners.

Neptune in the Sixth House

You understand the healing capacity of sexual intimacy. This simple statement deserves some thought. You have magnetic healing talent, and at no time are you closer to another person than when engaged in sexual intimacy. Therefore, pour your energy into your sex life, but not with just any partner. Developing a long-term relationship will deepen your pleasure while at the same time heightening your healing powers. Physical and mental realms merge for you during sex.

Neptune in the Seventh House

You may be satisfied with platonic love for extended periods of time. Sexual intimacy is not necessary for your overall contentment. However, you desire emotional closeness. To satisfy your partner, you will want to cultivate the capacity for physical pleasure yourself. Reserve times to be alone by yourself, and other times to be alone with your partner. Listen to your partner's idealistic yearnings. Share your own fantasies as well.

Neptune in the Eighth House

There's a lot going on in your subconscious where sex is concerned. You have great physical instincts. Follow them. Periodic bouts of self-doubt or depression can interfere with your sex life. It's best to address your moods directly because ignoring them won't make them go away. Meditation or any mental practice that focuses the conscious mind is great for your sex life.

Neptune in the Ninth House

Your foresight is visionary. When applied to your sex life, it allows you to anticipate your partner's needs and desires very well. This is great for your partner, but what about for you? Remember, your partner may not be as tuned in as you are. Verbalize what you want and need, or guide your partner's hand. You very likely will find that your partner is willing to respond to your direction enthusiastically.

Neptune in the Tenth House

You bring a nearly supernatural power into your sex life when you are with the right partner. You can be totally present and totally attentive in an intimate environment or in public. Be subtle. You may not want everyone to know exactly what is on your mind. On the other hand, be completely honest with your partner. Gather energy in public situations, and then take it home to the bedroom.

Neptune in the Eleventh House

You search for a soul mate with whom to share your life. You attract people to you psychically and must discriminate among potential sexual partnerships. Resist the temptation to hop in the sack with everyone who offers. Set noble standards for yourself, and adhere to them. This may mean fewer sexual partners, but long-term relationships lead to profound sexual satisfaction for you. Sex is one area where changing your approach works better than changing partners.

Neptune in the Twelfth House

You have bouts of pessimism where sex is concerned. Through experience you find that alcohol and drugs do nothing to enhance your sex life or your opinion of yourself. Instead, you find that you can use your psychic abilities to connect with your partner on every level of body and mind. You discover that you gradually slip into a state of intense ecstasy. There may not be fireworks. It's more like waves of feeling that build to a crescendo.

Neptune Aspects

Neptune's aspects reveal your receptivity on a psychic level. They indicate the natural direction of your spiritual impulses. Considered from the perspective of your sex life, Neptune's aspects indicate how you connect with another person to fulfill your spiritual and physical desires. In chapter 15 you can read about the aspects Neptune makes in your chart. Do you discover anything new about your own receptivity?

7
The Ascendant/Descendant
Self and Other in Intimate Partnership

The perception of self and other becomes blurred in sexual relationships. The union you seek with a partner can become so powerful that the usual ego boundaries relax and dissolve. When you are this close to another person, you are inside each other's auras. You feel like you are one unit for that brief moment.

The desire to merge becomes all powerful, and then ebbs as the desire to be completely independent takes over. As you separate, you regain the sense of your separate self, and you may even recoil a bit from intimacy. Feeling lost in the passion may not be comfortable in the beginning.

This ebb and flow of sexual energy makes for excitement in intimate relationships. You can enjoy sex without intense closeness. Even if you are not actively engaging in sex, you feel the tides of emotional attachment between yourself and any partner. As you understand your perception of self and other more clearly, you also develop ways to cross the boundaries to achieve more potent sexual pleasure. The signs on the Ascendant and Descendant indicate your typical style of sexual expression (Ascendant) and what you expect from a partner (Descendant).

Ascendant/Descendant in the Signs

Aries Ascendant/Libra Descendant

Your attention is always shifting. Your intuitive insight drives your actions more than any other rising sign. You are always introducing new ideas into the sexual mix and expect your partner to respond in kind. You achieve the best results when you introduce your ideas skillfully, considering your partner's feelings at that particular moment. Easing into a new format through conversation and foreplay will be delightful. Butting heads won't.

You expect your partner to be affable and adaptable. Your ideal sexual partner is cooperative and goes along with your ideas. He or she is also considerate of your moods and needs. When your partner is overly exacting about the process, you lose patience. When your partner is timid, you tend to push harder. When your partner vacillates, you tend to take charge. These tendencies lead to obvious dissatisfaction. Your best bet is to initiate sexual activity while considering your partner every step of the way.

Taurus Ascendant/Scorpio Descendant

Stability is a big deal for you. You want comfortable material surroundings that include old familiar furnishings. You desire to own your home or at least to have a lot of say in how it is arranged and furnished. You need to know what to expect when you engage in sex, and familiar surroundings satisfy part of that need.

You don't need total luxury to feel comfortable, but you do need familiarity. Oh, it's possible for you to enjoy sex on a camping trip, but probably not the first night out in the woods. You need time to adapt and settle in first. You like to be in charge of the plan so that you can provide all the things that make you comfortable and happy.

Where the actual sex is concerned, you anticipate that your partner will supply intense passion and significant staying power. You find that you warm up to your partner over months or years. You really like it when your partner plans a special sexual encounter, right down to the clothing, food, and drink. Then you can relax, lie back, and allow your senses to be stimulated. You like your partner to take control, and you may even like an impression of danger. You don't want real pain, though. Pain is a definite turnoff for you. You often expect your partner to supply more than 50 percent in bed.

Gemini Ascendant/Sagittarius Descendant

Your persona shines in a social environment. Sexual intimacy calls upon your ability to adapt to just one person. This shift can be daunting at times. Any superficiality will detract from the achievement of profound sexual satisfaction, and you know it. Therefore you may want to use your versatility by wearing a different mask when you are alone with your partner. You can still be lively and conversational. Just steer the sexual conversation and action in a focused way, avoiding any sidetracks. Make a mental note to bring up side topics later.

You expect your partner to demonstrate high ideals and principles in every area of life. This may not be the stuff great sex is made of. Your ideal partner is enthusiastic about sex. Your partner may think of sex as a sport, but it is a partnership sport, not a competition. Both of you will gain greater pleasure if sexual adventures stimulate your senses without causing any fear. Highly athletic experiments can be painful, so work up to those exotic postures!

Cancer Ascendant/Capricorn Descendant

Your personality reflects your moods openly. Sexual intimacy is one situation in which openness serves you well. You are able to let your partner know just what works and what doesn't. Water enhances your sexual experience, so don't be afraid to try the shower, the tub, or the beach—but maintain privacy, as that is a cornerstone of your feelings of security and safety. You like to sort of flow into a sexual encounter, easing your way to the most intense possible physical response. Your partner may prefer dry land for sexual encounters. The two of you can trade off, trying different arenas. Perhaps foreplay is better reserved for the water environment, or maybe the touch of ice or water on the skin acts as a stimulant for your partner.

Your partner may have a rather matter-of-fact approach to sex that doesn't satisfy your sense of flow all the time. When your partner wants to jump right into bed, you can get into the mood by spending a few minutes alone in the bathroom, changing into the proverbial "something more comfortable" in the way of attitude as well as clothing. You emerge ready for anything, and your partner will appreciate the effort!

Leo Ascendant/Aquarius Descendant

Where sex is concerned, you like to impress your partner and be impressed. Sex can become a big production if you let it. You enjoy luxury. This means that arrangements for your love rituals will include furnishing the setting richly and dramatically. You may spend an inordinate amount of time and money on bedroom furniture and décor. If you don't, you may find that your sexual appetite is stimulated in another part of the house, where your desire for luxury is satisfied more completely. When sex is good, it lifts you to a realm where you feel like you can accomplish anything.

Your partner is fully willing to try any sexual innovation you suggest. In fact, you may turn out to be the one who says no to certain sexual practices. Because your partner is always thinking about something, you have to make an effort to draw his or her attention to the subject of intimacy. If you contact your partner on the soul level as well as the physical level, you will achieve better physical results. Your partner's moods are more changeable than your own. You note your partner's diminished sexual endurance from time to time, unlike your internal fire, which continues to burn long after each sexual encounter. Your partner likes to talk about sex. In fact, you can talk your partner into a sensual state of bliss! If your partner is in the zone mentally, the physical part is icing on the cake.

Virgo Ascendant/Pisces Descendant

Even though you are very adaptable, you like a sense of familiarity and stability in your sex life. You can be your own worst enemy if you change partners frequently. When you do, you experience anxiety about health and security issues. You observe what your partner likes and file the details for future reference. You very much want your partner to give the same care and attention to your sex life. However, the thoroughness that serves you well in many areas of your life can turn into a clinical approach to sex. You like to play doctor, learning everything you can about your partner's body, emotions, and sexual desires.

Your partner is sometimes remote and lonely. You may find that you cannot make contact of any kind at times. To get through that level of reserve, you may want to plan for intimacy ahead of time, making a "date," if you will. This gives your partner time to work up to the moment. In this way feelings have a way of building to a higher pitch, making the sexual encounter profoundly ecstatic when it finally happens. Your partner benefits from your leadership where preparation is concerned; you benefit from the depth of feeling your partner can bring to any sexual encounter.

Libra Ascendant/Aries Descendant

Generally you are affectionate and pleasant with your partner. Even in your physical relationship you usually exhibit good manners. Problem: you don't like anything that even resembles dirty work. If you are overly fastidious where sex is concerned, you won't be able to enjoy the passion of the moment. In addition, you can't depend on your partner to make all the moves or come up with all the new ideas. It's very important for you to focus your attentions on one partner at a time. The depth of passion grows for you as you develop a sense of loyalty within the relationship.

Your sexual partner tends to be restless when things are too calm. Your sexual relationship thrives when you consider new possibilities and at least try things your partner suggests. Your partner is likely to be more impulsive than you, willing to jump in the sack at the slightest hint. If you disagree strongly, there could be angry fireworks. When the two of you agree, all the fire is concentrated in your physical relationship. How much better is that?

Scorpio Ascendant/Taurus Descendant

You flourish in steamy circumstances. Where sexuality is concerned, this does not mean hopping from bed to bed. It does mean sticking with one partner at a time and developing the relationship on every level, not just the physical. It may also mean having a plan for sexual encounters. Each time can be its own little conquest. Sex, for you, is inevitably associated with preservation of the species. You may select partners for their genetic nature as much as for love. You are intensely passionate in the bedroom and go more than halfway to ensure sexual fulfillment for your partner.

You seek a partner who appreciates a stable, comfortable environment. Owning your home can be a definite plus. You probably haven't associated home ownership with sexual pleasure, but think about it. Your partner can arrange the furniture and decorate to suit every sexual whim. A homey setting stimulates your passion too—as much or more than extreme luxury. While your passions run both hot and cold, you appreciate a more practical partner who takes care of the business of life. Your partner, to make you truly happy, must supply the warm, cozy, comfortable nest. Then your sexual passion can run wild in complete safety.

Sagittarius Ascendant/Gemini Descendant

Whether your life direction is toward social attachments or a more spiritual lifestyle, sexuality can be a big part of your regular regimen. You depend on the moods of others to dictate your actions to a certain extent. You tune in psychically to sexual undercurrents. Your fantasies—and actual experiences—may include sex on the ground beneath the stars, in the locker room, or in other atypical environments. Actions speak louder than words for you, so you don't require a long courtship to arouse physical desire. At the same time, your partner may mistake quick willingness for shallow feelings, and that is definitely not you.

Your partner is a social butterfly. This can make you nervous at parties, as you feel the sexual vibes and want to keep your partner for yourself. Jealousy can be attractive if it isn't carried too far. Your partner, however, may love to flirt, and this can drop you into a dark, unhappy mood. What you need is a partner who is a live wire, yet also able to adapt to your needs and desires without feeling cramped. While you don't need to talk to get into the mood, your partner probably does, so be ready to listen.

Capricorn Ascendant/Cancer Descendant

You tend to take the expedient route to your goals. Where sex is concerned, this approach works, but it may not have the spark that side trips generate. Foreplay can be an excursion all its own. You have a very strong will, and this aids in the physical control that makes sex especially stimulating. Remember, though, it's more about concentrating on the details of intimacy, and less on actually holding back from your partner. Sometimes you feel shy, even with a partner you know very well. When this happens, let your partner know that you need more time, or that now is not a good time. You are not obligated to have sex—it should always be a positive choice.

Your partner is probably more open about moods than you are. In fact, your partner may know about your moods before you do. The two of you find that even a moment's attention to the emotional mood can make or break the sexual ambiance. Your partner may enjoy taking long baths or showers with you. Getting hot and sweaty is no problem.

You attract partners who are hypersensitive to shifting emotional currents. You can't hide from such a partner.

Aquarius Ascendant/Leo Descendant

Your persona develops around the concept of independence. Yet the rebel mask you wear for others may be covering up your deepest soul urge for a stable relationship. Your partner may not be a mind reader. Logically, you know you have to verbalize your thoughts. You like to think of yourself as an innovator or reformer. Where sexual intimacy is concerned, your innovative spirit makes it possible for you to try just about everything at least once. You try it the second time just to be sure that your first impression was correct.

Your partner may not need a second impression. In fact, your partner tends to understand intuitively what will work between you. Your partner is probably more concerned than you are about the environment in which you enjoy sex. Take care to consider your partner's dignity, even when making wild, passionate love. Your partner enjoys an occasional adventure outside the bounds of your usual lovemaking style, so combine creativity with respect and you have an unbeatable formula.

Pisces Ascendant/Virgo Descendant

You have an abundance of feelings but may lack the inspiration to mobilize them. You desire a happy sexual union but are somewhat passive in terms of making the effort to ensure that happiness. For you, sex is best when you are in a comfortable relationship. It's getting to that point that can be difficult for you. You have at least one advantage: you are empathic enough to know what your partner wants. If you can overcome your own timid nature and use your receptive feelers, you can snag a partner who is on your same wavelength. Eventually, you want sexual pleasure, so be definite in seeking a partner!

Your partner tends to have a very methodical approach to life. Where sex is concerned, you are sometimes surprised about the attention to detail that goes into creating a sexual moment. You will find that you appreciate all that effort, and that you want to reciprocate. Allow your partner to take care of the details that don't even make your list of things to do. Exercise patience while the process unfolds. Remember, you benefit directly from your partner's ministrations.

Aspects to the Ascendant

Aspects to the Ascendant show the factors in your life that affect you most immediately on the physical level. They can be indicative of what stimulates you sexually. Because the Ascendant is associated with the physical body, you feel Ascendant aspects intensely. Read about your Ascendant aspects in chapter 15 to get a feel for your personal range of physical sensation.

8
The Midheaven/IC
The Role of Self-Awareness in Sexuality

Know Thyself. This axiom has stood the test of time in every arena. Where your sex life is concerned, it would be a mistake to assume that your partner knows what you want. Your partner may know what he or she wants, but cannot know what is in your head or heart unless or until you tell. You may not know what is in your head or heart either. You need to experiment a bit to find out what is most satisfying for you sexually. Then you need to be able to tell your partner what that is.

One reason you don't know yourself from the get-go is that your deepest desires arise as if from a well inside you. They are often hidden among other bits of knowledge that are only loosely associated with sexuality. Also, what seems like a good idea, once tried, can quickly get on your list of things never to try again.

Your astrology chart can inform you about yourself. Now you have information to help you understand your own sexual attitudes, desires, likes, and dislikes. You no longer have to test blindly until you find something that works for you.

As you pay attention to your inner urges and communicate them to your partner, you will find that the two of you both become more willing partners. You will know what your partner needs and desires, and your partner will know more about you. With this kind of knowledge, your sex life can become a powerful tool for personal and mutual ecstasy at times, and greater contentment between times.

The Midheaven and its opposite point, the IC *(Imum Coeli),* tell the story here. The Midheaven reveals both your sanity and any potential neurotic tendencies. The IC indicates what is arising from your deepest source. It includes your core beliefs—attitudes that can affect your sexual enjoyment and your ability to be with another person completely. As these core beliefs emerge, you get a chance to evaluate them, and to consciously accept or reject them. Sorting through beliefs is like crossing a minefield. You have to test each step to make sure it is all right to proceed.

You may find it helpful to read about the sign on your Midheaven, and then read about the opposite sign. The section on your Midheaven talks about what you can expect to arise from the less conscious realm in the way of beliefs. By reading the opposite sign, you can get an idea of what it would be like to have greater conscious awareness from the start.

The Midheaven in the Signs

Aries Midheaven

If you know anything about yourself, it's that you can be rash in your sexual activities. You want what you want, and you want it now. You rush into things without planning for every eventuality—in fact, you tend to omit the planning step completely, especially early in your sexual career. You have a less conscious urge to create balance in your life. Intuition can make you want to charge ahead without thinking. Proceed logically for better results. Moments spent in meditation help you discover deeper desires that can be met through a decisive effort to discriminate among all the possibilities open to you. Sound boring? Wait until you try this approach. You may be amazed at how your sex life improves.

Taurus Midheaven

You know your own strengths—and weaknesses. You don't need anyone to tell you your shortcomings. You also know the value of persistence. In your sex life you are able to keep going like the Energizer Bunny. The key is to know when to stop. If you were deprived in childhood, you focus your awareness on how to get and keep material things.

Your sexual partner is not a thing to be owned, so your protective strategies may not work as well in this area of your life.

Deep inside, you have a profound awareness of the ebb and flow of sexual energies within you. When you feel safe and secure, you can sense the flow of intense feelings in yourself and in your partner. As you access your sexual desire, you expand your perception of the material world immensely. Thinking less of personal gain and more of the power of sexual partnership, you achieve new levels of ecstasy.

Gemini Midheaven

Your mental powers are great, and you know it. You can usually think and talk your way through any situation. However, these two skills don't apply directly where sex is concerned. They help you indirectly by allowing you to communicate about your desires and those of your partner. You have a profound understanding of the impermanent nature of the world, so you make the most of each intimate experience. You learn to structure relationships without trapping either of you.

When you look deep within yourself, you find a limitless spiritual resource. When you act on spiritual impulses, you find you maintain an open mind and overcome any neurotic tendencies that once arose when you felt stagnant or closed in. As your spiritual capacity grows, you find that the familiarity of a long-term partner is beneficial in every area of your life, especially your sex life.

Cancer Midheaven

You wish to establish yourself as an individual in the world, and you may do this in your sex life by holding back something from your partner. This is not a matter of not loving your partner. It's about your desire for independence. Logically, the desire for protection suggests that you need to develop a sense of safety within your sexual life. Another area you know well is your capacity for stormy emotional outbursts. Sometimes you feel very out of balance, like the wave on top of rough water. You also know, though, that you have greater depth, like a mountain lake.

Deep within you is a well of self-confidence that has developed over years of experience. You have the capacity to work and keep working toward personal goals. What does this have to do with your sex life? Everything. Bottom line: you don't expect peak sexual satisfaction from the start. You are willing to apply energy and time to creating intense passion in your relationship.

Leo Midheaven

You want to be treated like royalty. You don't mind being put on a pedestal and worshipped. However, you know that isn't the real you. You desire to lead, and to become a self-confident, generous leader. Therefore it's best if your sexual partner allows you to take the lead at least part of the time.

Your inspiration for leadership in physical intimacy comes from a deep desire to assert yourself. You may read up on different sexual techniques and devise ways to try them out with your partner. You love the element of surprise, although you don't wish to be surprised yourself. You can expend a lot of energy in the planning, only to find that the technique falls short of expectations. You're amazed when you occasionally find that your partner is simply not in the mood when you are.

Virgo Midheaven

You know that order is of major importance in your life. This can make partnership difficult because no one wants to have all their actions measured against your relentless neatness meter. Intimacy can start out tidy and orderly, but clothes get rumpled and the sheets get crumpled in the process. You learn that emptiness is more to be feared than messiness, and then you focus your skills to create an intimate ambiance in which you can make whatever mess seems appropriate as you engage in sex.

Within your heat lies an ocean of feeling. As you look deep within yourself, you find that material objects have far less meaning. You also find that sexual intimacy provides a channel for your spiritual growth. Your outward fussiness masks your compassionate nature. You have experienced pain personally, and you know how to alleviate pain in others. The flow of emotions that occurs during sex heals you and your partner, so you feel connected to the universe.

Libra Midheaven

You understand your own need for cooperative relationships. You want to be kind and appreciative of others. However, when a relationship begins to fall apart, you are likely to become impatient with the process or indecisive about what direction to take. You also understand the importance of environment to your own moods. Your sex life flourishes in beautiful, harmonious settings. One of your greatest strengths is the ability to move between conflicting energies smoothly, maintaining your own balance. Because sex involves extreme passion, you may be disoriented by sexual excitement.

Passion and compassion both reside deep in your being. Another central instinct is to discriminate among your choices, finding the ones that are actually good for your spirit. Your sexual partners must stand up to this rigorous inspection, even if you are not consciously aware of it. Outwardly you are logical and rational, while inwardly you are running on the fuel of intuition. You have to tell your sexual partner what is on your mind.

Scorpio Midheaven

You know just how ruthless you can be about getting what you want. Your sexual escapades may be exciting, but in the end you realize you hurt yourself when you sink into sexual excess. You learn to choose your direction and emphasis more carefully as you gain experience. You also learn the value of dedicated, long-term devotion to one person. You exert less energy in anger and reserve more for cultivating transformative energy between the two of you.

Your deepest resources grow out of an expansive awareness of how the world actually works. You are seldom fooled by appearances, and when you are, you are stunned. You instinctively protect what you perceive to be your territory. It's best if you have a room all your own, where no one bothers you unless invited in. This space can be furnished with whatever makes you feel comfortable—you don't have to please anyone else.

Sagittarius Midheaven

You understand the value of careful planning. It's not so much the details that you decide ahead of time—it's more the broad spectrum of destination, along with a sketch of the path. Your sex life definitely benefits from some planning, yet sex occurs in the present moment, not the future. Therefore you have to shift gears in order to get the full enjoyment. Your have definite opinions where sex is concerned. Your partner will have to do some fast talking to get you to change much. You are adaptable, though, and can handle sexual changes one at a time.

Within your heart you have a mechanism that allows you to weather emotional storms well. Your attitudes soften when you understand the emotional dynamics of a situation. Every sexual encounter adds to your base of knowledge. Sometimes you are surprised when memory of a previous intimate situation pops up during sex. You have good instincts for pacing your sexual activity.

Capricorn Midheaven

You may think you already know everything there is to know about sex, or you may want your partner to believe that. You only change when you can see the practicality. You have truly remarkable self-control. When you choose to exercise it in the sexual arena, you can bring yourself and your partner to extreme peaks of physical pleasure.

On the inner plane, you are focused on your own soul's development. Your intense attention to the physical side of sex usually goes hand in hand with expanding spiritual communion with your partner. As your capacity for physical pleasure grows, your capacity for spiritual awareness also expands. When you direct your creative impulse to improving physical sex, you are in for a long run of sexual satisfaction.

Aquarius Midheaven

You are all about effective action. If you do something, you want to do it well. Sex is something you can master only through experience. However, you don't necessarily need lots of different partners to teach you. What you need is sustained, focused effort, preferably with one partner who appreciates your fears as well as your strengths. One potential fear is the lack of permanence in a relationship. If you let this fear dominate, then you may bring about the end of relationships through your own actions.

Deep within you is an intuitive voice that is always there to guide you, if only you will pay attention. When you are first getting into a relationship, that's a really good time to listen to your own guidance. If something doesn't feel right about a potential partner, save yourself a lot of grief. Don't go down the path of sexual intimacy. On the other hand, when everything looks right on the outside and feels right on the inside, go for it and don't look back.

Pisces Midheaven

You have personal drive on the one hand and an urge to serve on the other. You are probably more aware of one of these than the other. Where sex is concerned, you will not be truly satisfied until you can accomplish both personal satisfaction and the satisfaction of your partner. You also hate to give up anything, so the end of a sexual relationship can be extravagantly painful for you. If a breakup should occur, you are one person who may benefit from simply sinking into the pain for a while.

Deep in your heart you are a most orderly person. You seek to satisfy your sexual desires and sometimes worry that you won't get enough. Then you are stingy with your partner—not good. It's better to be as unselfish as you possibly can, all the time. Then you know you have made your best effort, and you also create ample space for mutual satisfaction to occur.

Aspects to the Midheaven

Aspects to the Midheaven indicate how you learn about yourself. They show the areas of your life and the kinds of energy that help you grow the most. They also indicate where you can mobilize your own will to improve your life on every level. As you read in chapter 15 about aspects to your Midheaven, think about how the interpretations offer insights into your thoughts, feelings, and behavior.

9
The North and South Nodes
Do You Have Sexual Karma?

Each of us has some karma to work out in the sexual arena. Whether from past lives or previous relationships in this lifetime, we each have experienced pleasure and pain to some degree. We each have successes and failures behind us in the romance and sexuality department.

Intimate relationships help us by revealing our weaknesses and flaws, but also by showing where our greatest glory can be found. Astrologers look at the North and South Nodes of the Moon—the points where the Moon's path intersects the path of the Earth around the Sun—to identify karmic themes of all kinds. Intimate relationships are among the most direct and poignant ways to discover your own karma.

When dealing with a partner, it's important to realize that your karmas may collide, but they are not identical. Something brings two people together. There's a sensual spark that ignites your inner fire. If that spark was struck in a past life, you may have some very old business to take care of as you engage in a sexual relationship now.

The North and South Nodes are always exactly opposite each other, and are discussed together. I feel it is important to think of the nodes not as a polarity that you see as either black or white, but as a continuum of possibilities. Sometimes you will identify very strongly with the North Node's sign, and sometimes you will find yourself immersed in the South Node. This reflects your pattern of sexual desire well—sometimes you are the assertive partner, and sometimes you are willing and even glad to be on the receptive end of the action. Sometimes you and your partner are so well-balanced that you can't tell which of you is assertive or receptive. There are myriad levels of variation between the extremes, and you will want to explore the range fully within your sexual relationships.

It's helpful to know where your partner's nodes fall. In the case study in chapter 16, the partners have reversed nodes: one has the North Node in Aries, and the other has the North Node in Libra, the opposite sign. This makes for a certain consistency in the flow of desire, even though the signs are opposite each other. When the nodes of the two people are in a different pair of signs, their motivating desires are different, and therefore the path to profoundly satisfying sex is different for the two partners. This doesn't mean that there can't be satisfying sex. It does mean that the partners must become aware of each other's path through experimentation and observation.

North Node in the Signs

North Node in Aries

You seek strong associations in every area of your life. Sexually you want a strong, vital partner, but may be astonished when you find one. When two dominant types come together, there can be major sparks. In past lives you may have played the dominant role sexually, but it's more likely that you have experienced subjugation. Now you find that an overly aggressive partner is stimulating, but frightening at the same time. Basically you want to be in charge of your sex life, but are attracted to dominating types.

You bring a fiery spark to sexual intimacy. Innovation is the spice of your sex life, and you are the one to bring new experiences to your partnership. Your partner shows you the potential for seeing beyond the physical satisfaction. Where sex is concerned, what you think is a very big part of what you get. In the past you have been all about thinking and not very much about acting on your impulses. Now you want to inspire your sex life so the two of you reach new heights.

North Node in Taurus

Birth and death are major themes that pervade your sex life. Your sense of personal values may get caught up in your assessment of your sex life. You know that sex is not all there is, but you want it to be satisfying. You may run up against the realities of pregnancy and child rearing as you explore your sexuality. Physical passion is not totally separate from procreation, but it is not necessarily bound to it completely either.

The cycles of life are a reality to be dealt with. Death connects to sex at the point where you surrender control. You could say there is a little death of the ego when you completely surrender.

You help your partner appreciate the growth of passion as well as the benefit of a comfortable setting. Comfort and safety make it possible to let down your emotional shield and surrender to the pleasure of the moment. Your partner can take you out of the ordinary to the transcendent edge of ecstasy. In the past you were the vehicle for your partner's transcendence. Now the tables are turned.

North Node in Gemini

Your sexual karma is based upon mental constructs. Your thought processes come into play when you converse with your partner about what you each want from your sexual experience. You seek out the facts. You always want to know more, but your conversation may lack depth. You seek broader experience, sometimes at the expense of intensity. Your partner seeks profound knowledge. However, your partner may focus on the philosophical ideal of sex and neglect the nitty-gritty physical connection.

Where sex is concerned, one goal is the ultimate physical experience. You help your partner experiment with something new and different. Your sexual partner reminds you to focus, sustain, and build spiritual passion. In the past you have been the philosophical partner. Now you are the conversation and idea person. Let philosophy take care of itself!

North Node in Cancer

Responsibility is a major theme in your sex life. Oh, joy! You have to be responsible about sex. This may not be your idea of a good time at all. Think about it for a moment, though. Meeting your emotional needs is an important part of the sexual experience.

The spiritual connection affects the flow of physical energy between you. In acting responsibly, you establish a deeper, stronger emotional attachment.

There is also a focus on social structures and laws, another fun area for sex! However, when you pursue a structure for your relationship, you discover that physical closeness with your partner outside the bedroom provides the necessary contact for you to feel more secure. The key is to develop a safe environment largely for selfish reasons.

Your role now is to help your partner build a secure nest. In the past you sought to draw your partner outside the security of the nest to experience the heights of passion. Now you appreciate the nest itself.

North Node in Leo

Your personal karma resides in groups. Your old business may include sorting out private, intimate activities from those more appropriate for the communal setting. In the past you were all for group activities, but that is no place for intimate sex.

You are warm, generous, and creative. These qualities serve you well in preparing for sexual pleasure. In the past you may have been cooler, more aloof, yet cooperative with your sexual partners. Switching roles may take some practice, but you can become a skillful initiator when your actions come from the heart.

You need to achieve balance between your individual desires and your group responsibilities. Group activities may dominate your career, for instance. In the past you wanted to be intimate with the whole world. Now the focus is on just two people. Help your partner form a deep personal relationship with one person—you. You intuitively know what your partner is thinking. Your partner brings rich imagination to the bedroom.

North Node in Virgo

Karma flows around issues of matter and spirit. In both cases you tend to get caught up in the details, and may fail to see the broader picture. If you focus too much on physical satisfaction, you may never reach the level of spiritual ecstasy, and vice versa. Your goal is to achieve a "perfect" sexual union on the physical plane. You therefore focus on material matters that affect your sex life. Health issues sometimes cause interference or require attention in order to reach physical satisfaction.

For your partner, the goal is to achieve a "perfect" spiritual union through sexuality. In a past life you have achieved spiritual bliss. Sometimes you fall back into that pattern, to the detriment of physical passion. Because you understand the power of spiritual ecstasy, you can now cultivate the physical side of sexuality, thereby empowering both of you to fulfill the spiritual expectation of sex.

Your partner helps you transcend fear. You help your partner maintain a strong physical bond.

North Node in Libra

While your partner is linear and direct, you seek balance. The linear approach can take you way out on a limb with your emotions, a place where you may be intensely uncomfortable. After all, sexual completion is about orgasm, and orgasm can feel very out of balance. Actually, sexual fulfillment brings every part of your being into harmony and balance through surrendering limiting concepts.

Your karma involves experiencing extremes of passion, while also preserving a sense of balance. In the past you have been the one who was assertive, or perhaps even aggressive, in sexual encounters. As the recipient of your partner's aggression, you now must learn to accept what you can, communicate about your insecurities, and develop trust in your partner.

You teach your partner not to forget the beauty of the sexual act. Your partner teaches you the sexual potency of direct action.

North Node in Scorpio

While your partner is all about comfort, you are all about risky behavior. You are willing to push your sexuality to the edge, maybe even over the edge, in order to experience extreme pleasure. The challenge is to examine what is important to you in terms of personal and family values, life path, and stability before you push the envelope of sexual experience. You like being in control, so the surrender of sexual passion requires a lot of faith in yourself and in your partner.

Your partner demands stability before sex can become fully satisfying. There is a sense of building your sexual partnership in much the way you would build an actual physical structure. Your partner is quite attached to the illusion of structure and permanence. Sexual passion meets resistance because the physical feelings are transitory.

You help your partner experiment with the pulsating nature of sexual passion. Your partner provides a stable container for your extremes.

North Node in Sagittarius

Perhaps your greatest strength is the capacity to draw together disparate threads of your two personalities to create a mutually satisfying sexual package. You connect experiences from daily life, spiritual leanings, and even thought-provoking items in the news to create a rich sexual ambiance. When you pull this off, you and your partner pass through the veil of apparent limitation and enter a world of higher aspirations.

Your partner is curious about your every thought and action. Sexual encounters can be playful interludes in which your partner comes across as much younger and freer than you expect. Sometimes you feel that your partner doesn't really listen to your input—he or she doesn't seem to get the whole picture, which to you is very important.

You help your partner find profound meaning in each sexual encounter. Your partner brings a breath of fresh air to the sexual relationship.

North Node in Capricorn

You like to think you are all about business where sex is concerned. You get right down to the "touch" part of the process and seem to overlook the feeling side. You rarely feel that your emotions are being overlooked in favor of mere physical exertion because your partner loves to take care of you and pays attention to your moods. You think you are able to take care of yourself, though.

Your partner seeks warmth and is willing to go more than halfway to ensure this part of the sexual contract. Be sure to find out what your partner wants, and then apply yourself to fulfilling that desire. Something for you to keep in mind is that your partner likes to be the one to satisfy your every desire—to create the emotional flow that can lift you to a new level of passion.

You teach your partner self-reliance. Your partner teaches you the value of emotional flow and release.

North Node in Aquarius

You tend to be a bit aloof. To get into the mood for sex, you sometimes require assistance. Your mind is occupied with thoughts about humanity in general. Your expectations of sexual pleasure may include fantasies about group sex or public sex. The inherent conflict in sexual relationships for you lies in the dichotomy between your focus on the larger group and your partner's desire for all the attention. Even more importantly though, to achieve sexual satisfaction you need to focus on your individual desires and on your partner's.

Your partner seems to open to you completely, while paradoxically demanding to be the center of attention. Between the two of you, the creative potential is vast. One way to achieve sexual fulfillment is to take the intellectual path. High ideals are not the stuff of practical activity, but they can be exactly what you need to create the mood for sexual passion.

North Node in Pisces

You slip into the connection with your sexual partner very easily—you can achieve a powerful psychic connection with anyone who gets that close to you. Thus you need to make sure you want to be that close to a person before you engage in sexual activity. The psychic connection amplifies your physical pleasure when the conduit is clear and there is mutual agreement.

Your partner analyzes your sex life in great detail—perhaps too much detail for you. Too much information shuts down your emotional flow. While it is easy for you to enter the psychic space, your partner needs encouragement in this area. If this is the case, you have to develop an atmosphere of safety and security so your partner becomes willing to open the psychic link. In fact, you have to develop this atmosphere every time you have sex.

You offer your partner the opportunity to form a profound psychic connection. Your partner teaches you how to organize details in service of the sexual relationship.

North Node Through the Houses

North Node in the First House

One of your biggest challenges is to accept your partner not as a reflection of yourself, but as part of yourself. You may seek a partner who will fulfill a sexual role that is a projection of your own fantasies. The partner is almost doomed to failure because your fantasies are constantly changing. Only the most unusual partner can keep up. In addition, your partner has his or her own agenda at work, and those fantasies may not mesh easily with yours.

Your challenge in any relationship is to express your fantasies verbally. Then when your fantasy shifts, your partner knows immediately. This may cause friction at first, but in the long run, passion will increase as the two of you share your deepest private desires.

North Node in the Second House

Your self-esteem is not simply a function of your sex life. Self-esteem comes first, and then you can have satisfying sex. You may think that self-esteem is about money and material things. That isn't the full picture either. What you think of yourself is your business and no one else's. You are responsible for developing inner strength and creating personal happiness, and then expanding that to include your partner and your sex life. Self-confidence and self-esteem allow you to pursue sexual pleasure more openly and directly. You also drop hidden agendas in favor of a more obvious plan.

North Node in the Third House

Your surroundings dictate your capacity to enter into sexual activity fully. Thus you have to consider and plan ahead. The setting of any drama dictates the possible actions of the players. If you want wildly exciting sex, then create an exciting arena. If you want languid, flowing passion, create that. If you want sex to be a trip, provide food, furnishings, and music to enhance the exotic feel of the moment. Be prepared to tell your partner a sexy story about what you have been planning.

North Node in the Fourth House

You are a genius at turning your normal home environment into a pleasure palace as you create a sexual encounter to be remembered. First, you may have to remove some of the ordinary stuff from your space—no messy laundry, piles of work, or other incidentals to distract you from physical pleasure. You may bring out soft flowing fabrics, and provide luscious tidbits of food and a good wine or other beverage. Include distinct flavors, like cheese, olives, or chocolate. Tantalize every physical sense as you create the stage for marvelous sex.

North Node in the Fifth House

You enjoy large social gatherings and may put so much effort into them that you have little reserved for the one-on-one intimate relationship afterward. Yet your sexual desire runs high. Balancing social and private relationships is an art. You can usually throw yourself into public situations easily. You may benefit from demonstrating a bit of reserve in public, and then engaging more deeply in your private sexual encounter. You and your partner can devise some truly creative settings or positions for intimacy. For example, find a place where you feel utterly safe and secure with the sun directly touching your skin. Hint: include sun block in your planning.

North Node in the Sixth House

The thrust of sex for you is wholeness. Everything you do to prepare and execute your sexual activity should contribute to the emotional and physical connection with your partner. What comes to mind is soft skin, trimmed nails, unwrinkled sheets, and possibly a scent you both enjoy. Make it easy for both of you to accept the other's ministrations and to surrender to the intimate connection between you.

North Node in the Seventh House

Sex is as much about your partner as it is about you—maybe more. Focus on your partner where sex is concerned. The more your partner enjoys you, the more enjoyment you will experience. Your challenge is to gain a sense of completeness by merging with your partner sexually. The physical act of sex is not all there is to this kind of connection. You get more when you see your partner as more than a separate object. This provides the missing sense of fulfillment.

North Node in the Eighth House

You want more than physical satisfaction. To satisfy your soul urges, it helps if you convey them to your partner verbally. To fulfill your soul through sex, you also need to relinquish control. Surrendering to your passion may not always be easy, but when you let go of "me" and experience "thee," you transcend individual boundaries and experience union on the soul level.

North Node in the Ninth House

Transcendent values do have a place in your sex life. In fact, they have a very important place. You reach beyond the ordinary in every area of your life, and sex is no different. Well, okay, sex is different. Yet transcendence is possible with a partner when both of you dedicate time and effort to every aspect of the relationship. One-night stands are not the stuff of transcendence. This level of ecstasy comes with experience. You can bring your so-called lower physical passion with you—physical stimulus can provide the bridge to your best sexual fantasy.

North Node in the Tenth House

You seek tangible structure in your sex life. You want your sexuality to fit into the broader picture of career, family, and society. This means that sex is not a separate area of your life that you pursue outside your regular routine. Sex is best for you when it is integrated with your thoughts, feelings, goals, and beliefs. Will you make a career of enhancing your sex life? Perhaps not, but you can certainly include sexual pleasure on your list of things to do, though not in public, please. That would be too uncomfortable for your partner.

North Node in the Eleventh House

Your sex life, like it or not, has to be acceptable to your friends and associates. Wild antics and multiple flings do nothing to enhance your image. They may satisfy you at the moment, but you find you have to pay the social price later. You are interested in the love you receive from your partner. Consideration of his or her feelings should be an essential part of your sexual approach. Ponder what you hope for in a relationship. Then communicate that in words and actions to your partner.

North Node in the Twelfth House

You have tender feelings that need to be nurtured and cared for in your sexual relationship. You seek to transcend the limits of the physical body in many ways. Sexual pleasure, being grounded in the physical, can be a bit of a contradiction for you because you are seeking emotional and spiritual bliss with your partner. Never think, though, that the physical part of sex is bad for you. Ultimate sexual satisfaction includes a burst of color and light that is beyond mere physical description, yet comes through intimate physical contact.

Aspects to the North Node

Connections between the North Node and the planets reveal how you form relationships with other people. Sexually these aspects show some of the easiest paths to intimacy. They also reveal how you are pursuing your life's mission through relationships. Go to chapter 15 to find interpretations for the nodes in your chart.

10
Mars and Venus
Individual Motivations

In sexual relationships there are two people. Regardless of gender, these two people are equals, or at least the sexual pleasure is better when they are equals. Each person has Venus and Mars in the chart. These two planets indicate how you attract others (Venus) and how you maintain independence (Mars). The two functions are not opposites—they are complementary. The positions of Venus and Mars in your chart show how you personally tend to work out the complementary energies. You may be more on the "Come here, come here" side of the coin, or you may be more "I'm here—now let's get it on!" Learn about your own relationship to these two planets, and then consider what's happening for your partner. You may not be able to satisfy every desire every time, but you can learn a lot about where your desires overlap with your partner's just by looking at these two planets.

Viva la Difference

Venus is all about attraction. We clean up, dress up, and enhance our appearance and personality in every possible way to attract other people to us. Venus also shows where and how we can become devious and deviant in our efforts to attract a sexual partner. For your sex life to reach the ultimate heights, you probably will want to focus your efforts on attracting partners that appeal to you in every way, not just sexually. This means employing discrimination in how you go about drawing others to you.

Mars is all about the energy of engagement. On the positive side, it's good to enter a sexual relationship enthusiastically and energetically. You want to warm up to the situation and join in actively. You want to feel the power of the moment. The undesirable side of Mars involves brutality. Hardly anyone enjoys being physically injured. Your partner doesn't want to be destroyed emotionally, or mentally either. Most of us enjoy an occasional surprise, but not a continual string of shocks and emotional upsets.

Venus and Mars contribute to better sex through the cultivation of mutual devotion. When the magnetism works both ways, the chemistry is fantastic. Physical heat and sexual passion arise as your bodies hone in on each other. Glandular functions inspire physical response. Can sexual satisfaction be far behind?

Venus in the Signs

Venus in Aries

You are a passionate lover. You create romantic fantasies and make them come true through your creative talents. You are an adventurous lover and may cause yourself problems if you stray from your partner. You definitely believe in love at first sight.

Venus in Taurus

Your power of attraction is very practical—you just "be" and it happens. Your partner can wow you with gifts of diamonds (or your favorite gem), but can also impress you with his or her attention to the practical dynamics of creative sex.

Venus in Gemini

Charm is your middle name. Even in the midst of wild physical sex, you can say the nicest things or smile just so. This requires no conscious effort. Able to adapt to your environment, you may find you are willing to engage in sex in circumstances that turn off your partner.

Venus in Cancer

Your feelings of love sometimes change into dependence. When you overexert in any area, your digestion suffers. While it wouldn't seem that your sex life could cause indigestion, it is wise to keep all your passions within limits so that you don't get an upset stomach. Let art and music set the tone for ecstasy.

Venus in Leo

You give new meaning to the term social butterfly. You love to dress up and attend luxurious parties and entertainment events. Your partner primes the pump for sex by showing you a good time on the town first. One thing to avoid: jumping into marriage too quickly. You want a love that lasts.

Venus in Virgo

You tend to let practical considerations get in the way of your lovemaking plans. You are indecisive about love matters and may miss opportunities to form lasting unions. When you develop a relationship step by step, paying attention to each nuance and change, you are more likely to end up with a fulfilling sex life.

Venus in Libra

You know how to enjoy yourself. You like social events and demonstrate good taste in your attire, friends, and other choices. You really like to be nice to everyone and this can result in spreading your resources too thin in the sexual favors department. You don't have to say yes to every potential partner.

Venus in Scorpio

Your sense of mystery acts like a sexual magnet, drawing people of both sexes to you. Sometimes overly controlled and sometimes way too loose, your experience wild swings in your sex life. You can be fanatical about a sexual partner. Any risky sexual activity can lead to illness.

Venus in Sagittarius

You imagine the most exotic and wonderful sexual encounters, and can be disappointed by the messy quality of the real deal. Your idealism makes it a challenge for your partner to achieve the pedestal status you outline for him or her. Other factors in your chart can provide stability in your sex life.

Venus in Capricorn

You want loyalty and faithfulness. Nothing ruins your sex life like finding out your partner has been with someone else. You like a mature partner—someone who knows the score where sex is concerned and is willing to teach you. Later you will become the teacher. Learn to surrender control.

Venus in Aquarius

You have very liberal ideas about sex. This doesn't mean that you personally have to act on your ideas, but you have a "live and let live" attitude in this arena of life. You also love your independence and don't want to give it up for the sake of a sexual relationship. You see the act of sex as an art form.

Venus in Pisces

You can be seduced by your lover, and you also are capable of seducing others. Your pleasant demeanor and sociability put you in the path of many potential partners. You must develop discernment if you are to avoid disappointment in intimate relationships. A tip for Venus in Pisces' partner: don't act like a mechanic. Instead, act as if each sexual encounter is a social event just for two.

Venus Through the Houses

Venus in the First House

Your head is your most attractive feature. Spend time getting ready for sexual activity by arranging your hair and removing heavy make-up and replacing it with something light and nearly transparent. Add items of jewelry that draw attention to your ears or to your hair. Consider the lighting in the environment so it emphasizes your face to good advantage.

Venus in the Second House

Your neck and upper chest reveal a lot about your feelings when you enhance them. Dress for the sexual occasion. You may want to wear nothing but your gold necklace or a gemstone that accents the shape of your jaw or throat. Cultivate a certain tone in your voice when you engage in sex. Then you can use that tone on your partner in other situations to stimulate sexual interest. And don't forget the back of your head and neck—they are just as sexy as the front!

Venus in the Third House

The chest and abs are focal points for sexual attraction. Choose clothing to accentuate a narrow waist or emphasize the bust line. Belts are an accessory that can be chosen to draw attention where you want it. Bathing attire naturally reveals the beauty of this part of your body. Your ribs may be particularly sensitive to touch.

Venus in the Fourth House

The chest and abs are focal points for sexual attraction. Choose clothing to accentuate a narrow waist or emphasize the bust line. Belts are an accessory that can be chosen to draw attention where you want it. Bathing attire naturally reveals the beauty of this part of your body. Your ribs may be particularly sensitive to touch.

Venus in the Fifth House

Your back and sides draw attention to your powerful musculature—definitely a sexual turn-on. Clothing that enhances the back has to be chosen with great care, as most clothing focuses on the front. The line of a dress, the pattern of a fabric, or the exquisite fit of a jacket or suit can do a lot to enhance the appearance.

Venus in the Sixth House

Physical attraction is below the belt for you, or at least below the ribs. If you are in great shape, reveal your tummy. Wear low belts to draw attention downward. If you are not in great shape, work out to develop this area. Choose clothing that not only looks good when you are standing in front of the mirror, but wears well for different activities.

Venus in the Seventh House

The lower back and hips are perhaps your greatest assets. The way you walk naturally draws the eye to your hips and bottom. Clothing that shows them off to the best advantage is a must. Lingerie doesn't have to be the most stylish. Rather, it should enhance your unique curves.

Venus in the Eighth House

This one is a bit tricky. You can't exactly go around showing your intimate body parts. However, your clothing can certainly emphasize what you have. Draping fabric tends to mold to the thighs and accentuate your sexuality directly. Tightly fitted pants draw attention to your bottom. Suggestion: patterned fabrics detract from the simple message.

Venus in the Ninth House

You are all about hips and thighs. Clothing that shows off your powerful legs will be sexually stimulating. The lower back is another area that draws attention. The act of dressing or undressing can focus the eye on these areas, so don't discount the power of a good striptease.

Venus in the Tenth House

Your knees may be your most attractive features. We don't usually think of knees as being all that attractive, but yours are. Clothing that fits closely to the knee or that reveals the knee will have sexual impact. Hint: if you are not out for sex, cover your knees.

Venus in the Eleventh House

Your calves and ankles are sexy. You could wear a dress that touches the floor, and in the moment when you sit and cross your legs, the glimpse of an ankle can be a remarkable come-on. Ankle jewelry is a good idea for you. Shoes should be chosen carefully, both to protect your ankles and to reveal their charms.

Venus in the Twelfth House

You can make your feet into sex objects. Guys: you will want to choose shoes, sandals, and slippers very carefully, and attention to toenails is desirable. Ladies: you can go all out with nail polish, stockings, and shoes that emphasize the shape of your feet. This is an area where fashion can go straight out the window. This is about your feet, not what's in vogue!

Venus Aspects

The aspects of Venus reflect the way your sexual magnetism works. Depending on the aspects, you may not be consciously aware of the things you do to attract sexual partners. Be sure to read about your Venus aspects in chapter 15 to discover what you do to attract a partner, and how you do it.

Mars in the Signs

Mars in Aries

You have tremendous energy. This may mean that you have sexual stamina, or it may mean that you put everything into a single encounter. Either way, your independent spirit can cause arguments that detract from your physical satisfaction.

Mars in Taurus

You have all the staying power of a locomotive. You are the original "more is better" sexual partner. You find that you can go too far—most partners don't have the kind of sexual capacity you take for granted.

Mars in Gemini

You are ready and able to engage in sex just about anywhere, anytime. This can be nice for you, but promiscuity can become an annoying habit that is hard to break. When you want to be the strong, reliable partner, you can put on that mask. Sooner or later you may actually believe it yourself.

Mars in Cancer

Your emotions tend to steer your sex life. To have a satisfying intimate relationship, you need to steer your craft into the main current and avoid the eddies and traps that lead to stagnation. You are more impulsive and less enduring in your feelings toward your partners, who could be quite numerous.

Mars in Leo

Your physical energy reflects your self-assurance. Sex, for you, is an enterprising act. This means that you want to get as much of it as possible, and you relish variety. You are capable of loyalty in a relationship, but it's a lot easier after you have sowed your wild oats. Too much focus on yourself and too little on your partner can lead to a relationship devoid of authentic feelings. Your sexual function therefore benefits from the discipline of working with your partner. It's also beneficial to recognize when your energy is at a low. Then you can just hang out together.

Mars in Virgo

Neatness counts, and your energy is often directed toward creating an orderly environment. This applies to sexual activities. You may enjoy bathing with your partner, brushing each other's hair, and preparing for intimacy carefully. All that preparation is sexually stimulating! Your approach to sex can be somewhat methodical. To avoid a mechanical feel, develop a variety of scenarios for your intimate encounters. You might even make a list of choices and allow your partner to select one (or more) at random. Leave any criticisms for later.

Mars in Libra

Your enthusiasm for teamwork is a big advantage in the sex department. You view intimacy as a shared experience and are not happy unless both of you achieve a degree of satisfaction. Setting the mood can be perfected to the level of an art as you become familiar with your partner's sexual preferences. The perfume of bath oils or incense can heighten sexual response. You may enjoy the feeling of a fan on your skin or warm massage oil being rubbed into any group of muscles. The bedroom décor should include muted colors, soft edges, and soft lighting.

Mars in Scorpio

Physical satisfaction seems like it is a live-or-die situation—you must have your physical needs met in order to feel alive. You can be ruthless in your pursuit of sexual partners, and you can turn on them just as easily if they don't meet your standards. You sometimes waste your time and energy on meaningless relationships, but you are also capable of deep and abiding passion with a single partner. A tip for Mars in Scorpio's partner: it will seem like no amount of stimulation is too much. It can be verbal or physical—both are effective.

Mars in Sagittarius

Sex can be an athletic experience for you. Remember, though, that it is not a race to see who finishes first. It's more like a pair of people riding a tandem bicycle up a mountain road to a secret spot where you can "peak" together. This ride demands teamwork and enthusiastic, sustained effort. Extravagantly energetic moves may detract from the goal, waste your energy, and even destroy the mood. Reserve your energy for a second helping (or a third . . .).

Mars in Capricorn

You occasionally overestimate your sexual capacity. Yes, it happens. You'll feel better if you accept the fact that you can have a sexual encounter without having a Fourth of July level of fireworks. Sometimes just being in the same space with your partner can be enough. Usually, though, your sexual energy is backed by physical endurance and will. You are able to take yourself and your partner to the mountaintop of sexual pleasure. When you get there, it seems like the stars are spinning around you!

Mars in Aquarius

Your endurance is matched by a deliberate intention to culminate each intimate encounter with glowing success. You are not satisfied with mediocre results. You take an organized, cooperative approach to your sex life, making sure all the desirable elements are present before you start. Well, actually, you have started when you begin to get organized. Sex for you is, after all, an intense mental as well as physical experience. Don't allow innovation to result in superficiality.

Mars in Pisces

You relish a quiet, calm atmosphere for the beginning of any sexually intimate experience. Children or pets making noise can provide an unwelcome distraction from the important business at hand. Your interest in occult sciences can add some unique elements to your sex life. Special incense can set a specific tone. Meditating on particular images can get you and your partner into a different mood. No drugs or alcohol, please, as they only distract you from the physical impact of sex.

Mars Through the Houses

Mars in the First House

Your naturally aggressive nature can sometimes obliterate desire in your partner. You don't have to scare each other in order to enjoy sex. Your independent nature also interferes with mutual satisfaction if you let it. You may have to learn through experience that sex is a team effort, to be enjoyed together.

Mars in the Second House

Your sexual partner is not a possession, nor is the love you share. Your self-esteem soars when you satisfy your partner as well as yourself. Put some of your energy into creating a comfortable setting ahead of time, and provide food and drink. Then the two of you can focus on the physical essence of the moment.

Mars in the Third House

It's all about mobility to you. You can have sex riding horseback! Well, maybe not, but you are willing and ready just about anywhere. This can lead to scattering your resources, or it can lead to a fun-filled, exuberant sex life with a partner who is as adaptable as you are.

Mars in the Fourth House

Your sex life is likely to be as intense as the rest of your life. After all, you believe that if something is worth doing, it is worth doing well. You are somewhat moody, which can detract from great sex on occasion. Try to let instinct kick in to overcome temporary gloom.

Mars in the Fifth House

Your self-assurance makes you a confident, enthusiastic sexual partner. You understand the connection between sex and conception and do your part to avoid an unwanted pregnancy. There is almost no limit to your passion, but you need to consider your partner's limits.

Mars in the Sixth House

You are a methodical sex partner. You study the ins and outs of sex and have probably explored sexual avenues that most of us would never think of. Don't let routine get in the way of taking a sidetrack to please your partner or to capture the moment more completely.

Mars in the Seventh House

You want a partner who challenges you. Your energy lasts and lasts, so there may not be many who can keep up with you. You enthusiastically enter into sex as a team sport, with you and your partner on the same side, coming out winners every single time.

Mars in the Eighth House

Sex is about survival for you. You think you can't last until the next time, but you can. In the meantime, think about ways to make each and every sexual moment better than the last. Reach for the sun, moon, and stars—they are there for you when you avoid criticism and focus on partnership.

Mars in the Ninth House

You sometimes have to spin quite a yarn to convince your partner to try everything you think up. For you, sex is a contest, or at least an athletic event. Your enthusiasm will be appreciated, but don't overdo and cause any injuries. A healthy adventure is fine.

Mars in the Tenth House

Your sexual ambitions are the stuff of legends. However, sharing the details of your conquests will not win you favor with your partner(s). You may think you are better in the sex department than you really are. For the best results, try to bring your ego down to the level of reality.

Mars in the Eleventh House

You love freedom. Feel free to experiment with sex, as long as you respect your partner's needs and desires. Teamwork is good. Share the tasks of putting fresh sheets on the bed, arranging a private dinner for two, and undressing each other.

Mars in the Twelfth House

Allow love to grow. This will enhance your sexual experience immensely. Cultivate a private arena for sex. Don't feel you have to have the perfect décor from the get-go. Look for modern and antique additions to create the right sexual ambiance.

Mars Aspects

Aspects of Mars reveal your best, worst, and most direct sexual approaches. They show where your energy goes in any activity. They reveal the nature of your energy flow and can provide insight into your sexual desires. Chapter 15 provides insights about your Mars aspects. You may want to compare your Venus and Mars aspect interpretations, as these two planets work together to produce sexual sparks.

11
The Fifth House
Love Given

We first learn about our need to be loved as children. As we grow, we learn how to give love to others. Even tiny infants learn to respond in ways that demonstrate loving feelings. Your sex life is an adult outgrowth of your capacity to love other people and to accept love from them. The Fifth House in your chart reflects the capacity to give love to others.

Sexual intimacy sometimes has the natural outcome of producing children. Having a baby together is one way to demonstrate your love for a partner. Parenting is not so easy, though. Even when two people want to have children, the demands of parenthood are great. We are taught surprisingly little about parenting, and we have to learn through experience with each child, as each child is unique. If you decide to have a child and your partner later leaves you, then you alone may have to see to the child's needs. This can put a strain on your capacity to give love to a new partner.

Then we have the possibility of sheer lust. In the twenty-first century, we have all sorts of options for preventing or ending pregnancy, so we can become indiscriminate in our choice of sexual partners. After all, there is little risk of pregnancy. Why not have some fun? Because each time you engage in an intimate relationship with another person, you take risks:

- You risk being hurt emotionally if the other person doesn't share your feelings.
- You risk contracting a sexually transmitted disease. This is a significant risk, not one to be overlooked or minimized.
- You fail to establish a lasting relationship—one in which you can cultivate your love, learn how to give love in greater measure, and learn to receive love in return.
- You fail to maintain a stable relationship, and this inability may damage your nonsexual relationships.

I am not suggesting that you can have only one sexually intimate relationship in your entire life. I am suggesting that you consider your long-term goals in terms of partnership and family when you begin the dating process. Don't wait until you have crossed the sex line. Think about the rest of your life before you get to the intimate stage. That way you can make more informed decisions that you can live with later.

The Fifth House also relates to recreation, and in particular to games of chance. I believe that games of chance should be recreational. That means that gambling in Las Vegas should not involve the money for next month's rent or your children's college education. It also means that sexual intimacy is not in the recreational category because sex should not be a game of chance. Take your sex life seriously. Play the games outside the bedroom.

The sign on the Fifth House indicates how you approach your sex life from the perspective of giving love and pleasure to another person. Obviously, love is more than a Mars/Venus attraction. It is more than a magnetic attraction between two people. Love is not an obsession. Love is an outpouring of positive thoughts and actions for the benefit of another person. Positive, dynamic love for a partner has, at its core, an ample amount of self-respect and self-love.

The Fifth House is also associated with the back and spine. Sometimes our most powerful backers are the people who love us. In football, the linebacker supports the linemen. To say you have backbone means that you have fortitude—a quality that is needed in a loving relationship in the long run. The Fifth House is where you can learn about your personal creativity in all areas of life. Giving love is just one of those areas.

The Sign on the Fifth-House Cusp

Aries on the Fifth-House Cusp

If nothing else, your energy and enthusiasm make you very attractive. You have an intense sex drive. You want to satisfy your sexual partner as much as you seek self-satisfaction. You may need to slow down to accommodate your partner's pace. Any competitive urges should be left outside the bedroom door.

You don't like to take direction from anyone, even your sexual partner. However, your way is not the only right way to have sex. For the two of you to experience equal pleasure, you must learn to pay attention to your partner's sexual needs and desires.

Taurus on the Fifth-House Cusp

You take a practical approach to sex in all its variations. You want to be comfortable and you want to be satisfied. Where your partner is concerned, you are likely to take a practical, although not necessarily boring, approach. You try what has worked in the past, see if it works now, and innovate as needed. You would be wise to let go of methods from your past that don't click with your current partner. Gender issues aside, what works really well for you may not be so great for your partner.

Gemini on the Fifth-House Cusp

You bring lots of enthusiasm to sexual encounters. You are willing to try whatever your partner suggests, but you are likely to err on the side of caution with new techniques. You tend to think about what you do with your partner, and at times you can seem distant from the physical part of sex. You like to collect mementos of important events in your life. Keep your collection of sexual memorabilia in a very private place. You have a dynamite memory for what your partner likes.

Cancer on the Fifth-House Cusp

You are generous to a fault. You will work overtime to make sure your partner is satisfied. This is a very fine attribute in your secret sexual résumé. Sometimes you overestimate your capacity, and you need to be considerate of your partner's capacity too. You pay close attention to all matters of the heart. When engaging in sex, you want every level of your partner's mind to be satisfied. Generally you are confident that you can deliver the goods.

Leo on the Fifth-House Cusp

You have a powerful sense of self. You are so self-directed that you are not always the most open, enthusiastic sex partner. You very much enjoy romance and pursue love affairs enthusiastically. Your sexual capacity reflects physical and emotional endurance. You want sex to be part of any love affair. You work hard and play hard, yet you tend not to be competitive in the sexual arena. Your natural generosity makes it easy for you to give love to your partner.

Virgo on the Fifth-House Cusp

You believe in the economy of effort and seek to apply it in the sexual realm. For example, you don't like wrinkled clothing. The care you take as you remove each article of clothing can be a big turn-on for your partner. You are a quick study when it comes to figuring out what your partner likes. You are also dependable in your delivery. You leave little to chance where your sexual partner is concerned. Remember, clean and precise can be overdone.

Libra on the Fifth-House Cusp

You know how to cater to your partner. Lest this sound too much like being a doormat, remember that your partner wants it to be your idea. Therefore, don't be afraid to add inspiration to your sex life with something extravagant from time to time, or even something edgy. Of course, it has to be beautiful or artistic in some way. Be ready, when the moment comes, to cut to the chase—your partner is all about being direct and to the point where love and sex are concerned. Show that you appreciate your partner's appearance.

Scorpio on the Fifth-House Cusp

You have powerful sexual urges that can overtake you at odd moments. It's probably best not to attempt to act on all of these urges. Better to whisper in your partner's ear, stating exactly what is on your mind, than to make a scene in public! You are capable of extraordinary sexual feats (only you know exactly what this means). Use your emotional intensity to fire up your partner for physical pleasure. There is a healing quality when you focus all your energy on your partner's body.

Sagittarius on the Fifth-House Cusp

You are able to give love to your partner freely and expansively. Your sexual drive is a strong factor in other areas of your life, as sexual satisfaction brings balance into your creative endeavors. When you feel confident, you are able to pleasure your partner profoundly. When you lack confidence, you tend to turn inward, making your partner feel unloved. These tendencies lessen in long-term relationships because both partners understand the emotional ebb and flow better.

Capricorn on the Fifth-House Cusp

Your down-to-earth style leads to solid results in your sex life. You are willing to expend effort to satisfy your sexual partner, and you put in more than your 50 percent in love relationships. You may feel disappointed in love. You may feel that no matter how much you give, you are not getting back as much as you would like. You feel responsible for what happens in relationships, and therefore make a diligent effort to do your part. This can come across as fulfilling your duty, and not as enjoying the pleasure of sex.

Aquarius on the Fifth-House Cusp

Your sex life may include some steamy affairs. You care a great deal about your partner, and you use all your faculties to ensure your partner's pleasure—while you are interested. Then you tend to go on to the next relationship. Behind this partner-switching tendency, you really do want a long-term, loyal relationship. When you are in one, you contribute a lot of spark to each sexual encounter. It's important for you to find a sexual partner who shares your enthusiasm and who is willing to help you uncover any repressed feelings that intrude on sexual satisfaction.

Pisces on the Fifth-House Cusp

You tend to be very romantic, but not very realistic when it comes to love. You look in the wrong places, and you give your love to the wrong people. You may engage in all-or-nothing sexual extremes. Neither extreme is really good for your sense of self-worth, and your partner won't like this much either. Figure out what is imagined in your sex life and what is real. Where giving love is concerned, you can give your partner love and satisfaction in many ways, even when you don't have much enthusiasm. The tide will turn, and your enthusiasm will return.

12
The Eleventh House
Love Received

We all want to be loved. Everyone seeks fulfilling relationships of one kind or another. Yet the love we receive is largely outside our control. No matter how you try, you cannot make every person love you. No matter how you try, you also can't make everyone hate you. Like everyone else, you receive love more according to circumstances and less through personal effort, although effort is needed to sustain love. Let's look at four concepts related to the Eleventh House, and see how they relate to receiving love.

Idealized Love

We each have a fantasy about what love would be like if we got some of it. We imagine how wonderful we would feel, or more precisely how "it" would feel. The word "it" shows just how far removed any fantasy is from reality. The sign on the Eleventh House describes how you fantasize about love, and it tells you something about what you expect in a love relationship.

Your Stepchildren

Whoa! That's a switch! What do stepchildren have to do with receiving love? For one thing, if your partner's children don't like you, they can make it very difficult for the two of you to get together. That could interfere big time with receiving love and the sexual pleasure you expect from a loving relationship. Secondly, your partner's children represent his or her previous love relationship. They reflect the result of the gift of love. Pay attention to this bit of truth.

Group Admiration and Approval

The Eleventh House has to do with your relationship to groups of people. This is a bit more complicated where your sex life is concerned. Most of us stick to the idea that intimacy is a private experience. We don't put groups and sexuality together in the same thought. Yet we often find our partners through the groups we join. Many of us met our sexual partners at school, in church, or at work—all places where groups gather.

Mental Games

Finally, the Eleventh House relates to mental activity. We cast an idea out into the world, and we wait to see what happens with it. We make plans for the future so we will be prepared when an opportunity arises. We don't know when the chance will come, or exactly what it will look or feel like. Of course we hope we will like what we get. That sort of sums up how we feel about love—we cast our love out there sincerely, and we hope that we will receive something in return. It's best to love freely and not plan on that love being returned. Still, we always expect some positive result from our actions, and love is no different.

The following interpretations suggest ways in which you anticipate what it is like to be loved, and how you believe you will feel about sexual intimacy. Just a word to the wise: what you expect may not be anything like what you get. Remember a time when you expected to get dessert, and all you got was vegetables? Or you had to eat the vegetables first? How did that affect how you felt about the dessert? If you expect something sweet and warm in the sexual arena, and instead you get fiery and intense, how will that feel? Or vice versa? The thing to understand from this chapter is that if you expect sweet and warm, you need to convey that expectation loud and clear—preferably in both words and actions. If you want fiery and intense, suit your words and actions to that desire.

The Sign on the Eleventh-House Cusp

Aries on the Eleventh-House Cusp

You expect to experience the fullness and depth of love. Fullness and depth come with time. This suggests that one-night stands are probably not your cup of tea—impulsive sex is not going to satisfy you in the love-received department. Another thing you expect is for your lover to be organized. You don't want to be in charge of the details. You want your partner to adapt to your desires. If a certain lovemaking style doesn't work and you say so, you expect your partner to listen. By asking for one thing and discovering greater satisfaction with something else, you contradict yourself where sex is concerned. The best way to get your needs met is to show your partner what you want.

Taurus on the Eleventh-House Cusp

You have fairly progressive views about love, so you are open to receiving love from multiple sources and in different forms as long as you are comfortable in the process. Comfort means that the love you receive comes in a pretty package without any physical pain. You do have some strange ideas about sexuality, and you may plan intimate moments that don't deliver what you expected. In fact, too much planning can lead to rather boring results. You expect your partner to have above-average physical endurance. You also may find that you enjoy vigorous stimulation.

Gemini on the Eleventh-House Cusp

You like to think about love and sex, and you like to talk about it. You may achieve deeper levels of satisfaction when your partner talks during sex. Your inventive side expects your partner to come up with new techniques. The usual is not disappointing exactly, but you want to add some spice to your sex life from time to time. You expect your partner to be enthusiastic about trying this, that, and the other thing. You also enjoy sexual pleasure when you are alone. Because you need to love yourself in order to give love, learn what pleases you and tell your partner. Remember, talking goes both ways.

Cancer on the Eleventh-House Cusp

You expect your partner to divine your emotional state and mental attitude. This is a tough requirement. Your partner is only human, sympathetic to your needs, but you get better results when you say what you want. You probably don't anticipate the pain you will feel if your partner leaves you. Thus you have to balance your expectations. You want your partner to be fairly independent, but you want loyalty too. Tell your partner what you're in the mood for. Then sex can take its most pleasurable course.

Leo on the Eleventh-House Cusp

You expect your partner to know intuitively what's on your mind and in your heart, and what will provide you with the greatest sexual satisfaction. Unless your partner is psychic, you will be disappointed in love. You find sex titillating when your partner occasionally rebels against the normal course of lovemaking. You enjoy a certain amount of sexual contact in risky situations like public events. However, you probably don't go in for teetering on the edge of a cliff while engaging in sex. You want a partner who allows you to experiment. Remember, the appropriate boundary for experimentation stops short of actual danger and fear for almost everyone.

Virgo on the Eleventh-House Cusp

Remember the song about the partner with the slow hand? You want that sort of detailed exploration of your sexuality. This can include trying every possible position, but it also includes your partner serving a glass of wine and your favorite food, dressing impeccably, and undressing you methodically, appreciating every thread as it is removed. You don't want your clothes ripped off—you want them peeled off. Receiving love, you believe, should be all about pacing. You want it to build to a shattering climax, but you want to enjoy every tiny move on the way there. Your partner should talk about what he or she is doing too.

Libra on the Eleventh-House Cusp

You have some very imaginative ideas about love. Sometimes you find that actual sex doesn't match up with your somewhat sentimental ideas. Your partner can enhance your experience by making sure that intimacy is the ultimate in clean—fresh bed linens, perfumed body oil, and sensual lingerie add to the pleasure of all the senses. You can be teased into bed through stimulation of senses other than touch, especially if your partner pays close attention to your preferences. Your partner should be willing to bring the occasional strange sexual technique to the bedroom. In your imagination you have considered some very offbeat possibilities.

Scorpio on the Eleventh-House Cusp

You expect love to come to you in a powerful, potent package. Your partner must be physically aggressive in order to satisfy you. You may even be willing to feel some pain. Probably it is the force involved in the chase that you like, and not actual physical injury. Still, in the excitement you may get an occasional bruise. Beneath your expectation of aggression, you find that what you really want is enough energy to take you to a transcendent level. To get there, a lot of people find that a relentless approach works better than physical force. A partner who will sustain foreplay until you are trembling, and then "torture" you a bit more, is able to dish up the kind of sex you want.

Sagittarius on the Eleventh-House Cusp

A part of you is sexually greedy. You probably have had the experience of being very sore after passionate lovemaking. Another part of you likes the idea of being with your partner for many years to come Over time, you modify your sexual activity to suit different physical desires and limitations. The two of you evolve into a new style of giving and receiving physical pleasure. The depth of pleasure you seek does not develop overnight. Rather, long-term commitment allows the two of you to explore your mutual potential for satisfaction.

Capricorn on the Eleventh-House Cusp

You like a partner who concentrates on you and you alone. Whether you are out in public or in your private inner sanctum, you want your partner to take you seriously. You want your partner to be a reliable sexual partner too. You are willing to leave extreme sexual experimentation to others. Because you see love as an intentional thing, you don't relish surprises and may even prefer to select your own Valentine's Day presents. You expect your partner's love to grow on its own, without much help from you. This could be a mistake. To keep your love nest from becoming a desert, feed your partner with your emotional as well as your physical response.

Aquarius on the Eleventh-House Cusp

You know that your partner understands human nature. However, it may seem that he or she doesn't understand you very well. You expect cooperative effort in your sex life, and you get confused when your partner goes off on some rebellious tack, refusing to follow your lead. You are sometimes astonished by your partner's emotional response. While you desire the unusual in your sex life, and hope for special demonstrations of love, you are not so fond of your partner's strange tastes or desire for some new sexual experiment. Even though your partner's love is steady, his or her ability to change emotional direction on a dime makes your love life a roller coaster affair.

Pisces on the Eleventh-House Cusp

You have the power of magnetic attraction—you may attract potential sexual partners who don't meet your expectations. You search for a soul mate who will understand your every desire. You are a noble soul, but actually nobility is not what you want in your sex life. The love you receive should be filled with sensitivity. It will not depend on words alone. You want your partner to set the sexual stage with delightful bits of your favorite foods and flavors. Or you want to be surrounded by a variety of colors or textured fabrics. Being blindfolded may provide an interesting sexual experience.

Summary

By now you have seen just how differently you perceive love given and love received. You may start out expecting to receive love pretty much the way you give it. Yet your own chart says there's a profound difference between your style and what will satisfy you in return. To get the love you need and want, and to ensure a satisfying sexual relationship, think about the differences. Consider how important it is to understand what you desire at a deeper level.

Perhaps just as significant is what your partner wants. When your partner is satisfied, the chances are very good that you will get more of what you ask for in return. Look at your partner's chart to see what his or her expectations are in the love department. You can enhance your partner's sexual experience by paying attention to how your Eleventh House and Fifth House support each other.

13

The Eighth House
Sex, Shame, and Transformation

Each of us has sexual impulses. The fact that these impulses exist in tremendous variety is something most of us don't realize, at least not early in our lives. Variety begins to make its appearance as we become romantically involved with one or more partners and as we begin to explore our personal desires.

Sexuality is revealed through every part of the astrological chart. However, this chapter will focus on your sexual impulses as they are reflected in the Eighth House of your birth chart. The Eighth House is associated with the external sex organs, the rectum, and the sacrum. There is a physical association to venereal diseases and the urethra. The sex force itself is reflected in the Eighth House.

The Eighth House governs a few other important areas of your life—death and matters associated with death; dowries, legacies, and inheritances; surgery; dream consciousness; and financial matters associated with your partners. I have a reason for mentioning this list of other Eighth-House matters. It is not so easy to separate some of them from your sexual impulses. They may not sound like they are closely related, but they often are. Dreams are often filled with exotic, frightening, or just plain superb sexual experiences.

When we experience the death of someone dear to us, we may feel the need for sexual experiences. The sexual experience accomplishes a few things:

- It takes over our emotions and distracts us from the pain of loss.
- It reminds us that life goes on in spite of death.
- It provides reassuring closeness to our partner.

Death is part of the continuing cycle of life, and sexuality is integral to that cycle.

Your partner's finances can be a source of pleasure or pain. Emotions connected to finances can interfere with or enhance sexual satisfaction. A dowry or inheritance may make it much easier to create settings that lead to sexual pleasure.

While there could be a direct association between surgery and sexuality, particularly if the sex organs are involved, the connection is less direct most of the time. Necessary surgery prolongs life, and therefore involves the birth/death cycle in which sex participates. Elective surgery enhances life experience. It can make us more attractive, more mobile, and, indirectly, better sexual partners.

The fact is that any aspect of life influences your sex life. The matters associated with the Eighth House have profound effects on your achievement of satisfying sexual experiences.

Shame, and How to Eradicate It from Your Sex Life

I was once working with a Japanese student who had come to the United States to study dance therapy. This student was working on the concept of shame as part of her preparation to write her thesis. The thesis didn't involve sexuality directly. In the process of discussing the differences between the American and Japanese concepts of shame and guilt, we discovered significant cultural differences. Keep in mind that the social and cultural context affects your views about shame, aside from any astrological indications.

Astrologers associate shame with the planet Saturn. Unless Saturn is connected to your Eighth House in some way, you don't need to feel any shame where sexuality is concerned. However, many of us experience shame about one bodily function or another. Saturn and its aspects indicate where and how you may experience shame. Just by understanding the dynamics of your own Saturn, you may be able to resolve any shame associated with your sex life. When you read about Saturn's aspects in chapter 15, see if that triggers an awareness of how or why you feel shame. Then work on the structure of your sex life to compensate for those feelings.

Transforming the Ordinary into the Extraordinary (or the Sublime)

Once you have isolated Saturn and shame, you can tackle the Eighth-House objective of a more satisfying sex life. The mechanics of sexuality are such that you can have a sex life without having much satisfaction. With understanding, you can enhance your pleasure and satisfaction dramatically. The old adage "Practice makes perfect" can be applied to your sex life. No one I know had the best sexual experience the first time. We find more pleasure in skillful sex, and skill takes time and effort to develop.

The sign on the Eighth House tells something about the sexual impulse, and how it can be satisfied. This sign also suggests ways to achieve physical ecstasy.

The Sign on the Eighth-House Cusp

Aries on the Eighth-House Cusp

Your instinct for survival can be a sexual asset if you don't carry it too far. Sex is a win-win game. You don't have to destroy your partner to be satisfied—far from it. Harness your abundant sexual energy, and focus your attention on the pleasure you can share.

Transformation comes to you through intuition. You begin to see what the future can hold for you, and you strive to achieve that vision You can stimulate your intuition by heightening your physical response during sex.

Taurus on the Eighth-House Cusp

As you begin each sexual encounter, release your sexual magnetism, and mentally fill the space around you. Even while you still hang on to self-control, act as though you have lost it. Prolong the build-up to ecstasy, and then let loose with whatever wild behavior seems right at the moment.

Physical sensation can be an avenue to transformation for you. Pleasurable sensations can overcome pain. As you deepen the physical experience of sex, you reach within yourself to a transcendent source of love and life.

Gemini on the Eighth-House Cusp

Talk sex to your partner. Speak in a foreign language if you know one. Talk dirty. Avoid sarcasm, arguments, and criticism. Say, "I want . . .," and fill in the blank with a detailed description of exactly what will turn you on.

Your transformation comes through words. You learn to say exactly the right thing to your sexual partner. This skill transfers into every other area of your life, and you find the right words in just about any situation.

Cancer on the Eighth-House Cusp

You feel like life is a huge struggle and you need to fight your way through it. Sex is not about fighting. However, you can bring the same emotional intensity to your sex life. To get the best results, allow your energy to flow, like water running downhill. Let it go wherever it wants. It will lead to ecstasy.

Transformation for you is not an explosion of light—it's a gradually building, flowing experience. One moment you know you are the same as always, and then you flow into an entirely new experience of self, of your partner, and of love.

Leo on the Eighth-House Cusp

You actually have an excess of passion—no kidding. Use your willpower to channel all that energy into meaningful sexual encounters instead of dissipating it in meaningless acts. Cultivate a warm, sharing attitude instead of a "me first" approach.

Your transformative capacity is a bit like baking bread. At first there are separate ingredients to your passion. Then they are mixed together and allowed to rise. It's when the dough goes into the oven that the magic begins. Sustained sexual energy is the key to your transformation.

Virgo on the Eighth-House Cusp

Details, details, details. You want to understand every detail of your sex life, and you want to understand your partner too. It seems that the more you know, the more you grow in the ecstasy department. But remember, what works in the sexual arena may not apply to other areas of your life.

You experience transformation in your sex life when every part of your body participates. Ask your partner for a full body massage. Make sure every part of you participates in the building energy that physical touch engenders.

Libra on the Eighth-House Cusp

You are a master at perfecting your appearance to attract attention. You can look sexy or childlike if you want to. Don't expect the childlike look to attract the sort of sexual partner who can satisfy your adult needs. And don't reveal all your assets ahead of time—surprise can be a good thing.

You can imagine transformation and make it happen. What you think truly is what you get. You will have to practice using your imagination while also staying in contact with the physical sensations of sexual activity.

Scorpio on the Eighth-House Cusp

You are sexually suggestive with every word and every movement. You dress the part, and your partner loves it. Excess is not necessarily best here. Leave something to the imagination so your partner will be kept guessing for a while.

You understand transformation on a profound level, and you naturally know what brings you to the brink of intense passion. You are not afraid of the brink, but it takes you a while to process what happens in the explosive moment when you lose control.

Sagittarius on the Eighth-House Cusp

You want material things. You don't need every luxury, but what you want, you really want. You have big ideas about what you can accomplish, and you can overrate yourself in the sex department. Your craving for pleasure can lead to difficulties, so channel your desire effectively to reach the heights of ecstasy.

Transformation is a rather philosophical outcome. You want to be changed, yet you really like where you are too. Allow the fire of sexual passion to replace doubt with mental clarity.

Capricorn on the Eighth-House Cusp

You are so serious that your sex life may suffer. Your interest in metaphysics can help here. Study the sexual side of metaphysics for hints about how to transcend those melancholy feelings. You can be reborn into a higher spiritual experience of sex and pleasure.

How do you transform the rock that is your basis of behavior? You certainly don't want to be ground down. Instead, think of each sexual endeavor as climbing one step higher on a mountainside. You will eventually reach the top.

Aquarius on the Eighth-House Cusp

You are always pushing for more. Where sex is concerned, this can lead to licentious behavior that gets you little more than momentary pleasure. Avoid all dangerous sexual practices. Instead, cultivate your inner vision to help focus your sexual energy.

You don't have to have sex with everyone on the planet to make this a better world. Transformation can be an intellectual process, fueled by sexual energy

Pisces on the Eighth-House Cusp

You have an instinctive touch when it comes to sex. You experience sexuality on more than one plane, and hope your partner can go there with you. You may tend to close your eyes during any sexual experience. Try keeping them open to help you stay in the present moment.

Transformation for you is like the alchemical process of dissolving a lump of stone and reconstituting it as a gem. Sexual ecstasy dissolves you into a million pieces. When you come back together, you find that pain, sadness, and other negative emotions have shrunk or disappeared entirely.

14
The Twelfth House
Secrets, Less Conscious Sexual Urges

It's tough to hide when you are in a sexual relationship. We all have secrets of one kind or another. Some of our secrets are unknown even to us—our unconscious desires are just as potent and just as active as our conscious ones. Any relationship that lasts very long is bound to uncover some of our secrets.

An example is sibling relationships. For most of us, the longest-lasting relationships we will ever have are with our siblings. Brothers and sisters know us all our lives, and they often participated in the acts that gave rise to our secrets. Even if they did not, they know how we think, they can anticipate our actions, and they definitely have experienced our feelings, even if they don't understand how we felt.

When we enter into an intimate relationship, we often want to protect our secrets. Which of us is initially willing to reveal every flip and twirl of our previous love life? Not many. Even the boastful among us probably reserve some secrets. Yet as time goes on, our romantic partner discovers the facts.

Through your responses, you tell your partner what feels good and what doesn't. Even if you attempt to hide your true feelings, there is a subtle physical response. If your conscious and unconscious signals are inconsistent, your partner becomes confused about what you really want. Therefore, it's a good idea to understand your desires as fully as possible.

The sign on the Twelfth House reveals a lot about your secret self. Some of what you read here will be obvious to you. You may even think, "Sure I feel that way, but who would want to tell that?" You may read other remarks that seem foreign to you. This may be because you don't share that secret at all. It also may be that you are less conscious of that side of your own nature.

One way to evaluate less conscious secrets is to analyze feelings that surprise you. If your sexual partner causes unexpected pain or pleasure, it may indicate a less conscious factor. This is especially true if a person could reasonably be expected to respond differently. For example, if stroking a part of your body elicits fear instead of the expected pleasure, it may be that you have been injured and carry a less conscious memory of that time. The reverse may also be true. If you experience pleasure when a reasonable person could expect a pain response, you may be reacting to an experience when that kind of pain was somehow associated with pleasure.

It's important to mention here that some things are best left unsaid. Your previous sex life may have little to do with your current relationship. Boasting about previous exploits is not likely to warm your partner to you now. In fact, such remarks feel like comparisons, even if they are not intended that way. Sexuality is not a contest, and comparisons are not necessary or desirable. Each act of sexual passion provides its own satisfaction, independent of previous experience, even experience with the same partner.

Let's consider timing while we're at it. Some mention of past experience may be appropriate at some time in your relationship. Perhaps you recall an experience that you feel will benefit your partner in some way. Perhaps you recall an experience that is holding you back, and you tell your partner in the hope that you can overcome it, or you want to clarify your own hesitation or lack of response in the present moment. Perhaps you want to clear up old business to open your heart more fully. Each of these possibilities can be helpful at the right time.

The following descriptions of the Twelfth House may provide food for thought about your secret life. As you read about your own sign, consider which secrets may be safely revealed in the context of your sex life. Also consider your own less conscious motivations and instincts that affect your sexual pleasure.

The Sign on the Twelfth-House Cusp

Aries on the Twelfth-House Cusp

Enthusiastic though you may be about sex, you want this to be a private matter. You probably experience a lack of control where sex is concerned and have to learn how to dampen your sexual energy when sex is not an appropriate outlet. You may channel that energy into personal activities. You may occasionally succumb to alcoholic or drug excess, two ways to shut down your capacity for sexual pleasure.

You are interested in occult subjects. This interest can lead you to join organizations that explore esoteric subjects including tantric and other sexual rituals. You can be ruthless in pursuing sex. When you learn to gather sexual energy instead of dissipating it, you will achieve far greater heights of pleasure. And it can still be a private affair.

Taurus on the Twelfth-House Cusp

You could pine away thinking about the ideal lover. The importance of romance and sex in your life cannot be overestimated. When you are in the throes of passion, you lose self-control. This is not a problem, as long as you are in a private, secure location when you do so. You are so impressionable that the most unlikely characters can seduce you. The right atmosphere and a bit of encouragement can induce you to do things you could regret later.

On the positive side, you produce sexual encounters the way you would produce a movie. You leave no stone unturned to set the stage and create the desired ambiance. Love and sex are the stuff of your dreams, and you make those dreams come true when you have a strong partnership.

Gemini on the Twelfth-House Cusp

You are receptive to other people's suggestions. This is good when you trust your partner, but not so good when you are with less trustworthy companions. You have a dynamic fantasy life. Although this is largely a private matter, perhaps even secret, you occasionally allow your partner to share it with you. You may find that sexy magazines and movies give you a sexual rise.

You tend to overplan your sex life. You read about a sex game or see sexy pictures, and you fantasize about what it would be like to follow through on the posture or pose. The problem is, your fantasy includes an ideal lover who is completely pliable. Most of us do not have such a partner. To get the most from your sex life, verbalize your fantasies so your partner can join in directly and joyfully.

Cancer on the Twelfth-House Cusp

Your moods are subject to the emotional currents around you. Sometimes you don't know for sure if you're following your own desires or being led into fulfilling someone else's fantasies. You run the risk of unconditional surrender when you actually need to remain in control of your faculties. You need to develop strong values to help you in this area.

Try turning the tables in your sex life. Have your fantasies in privacy. Develop your secret desires by yourself. Then when you connect with your partner, you have a well-considered plan of action. Act out the role of the aggressive partner, and surprise your partner with the new you. There will be time later for you to take the passive role.

Leo on the Twelfth-House Cusp

Your love of comfort can be a strong ally in your sex life. You secretly plan and prepare for the best sex when you are first open to your partner's desires. Find out what turns your partner on, and then plan an extravagant event in which you magnify each desire to its pinnacle. Appeal to your partner on every possible level of experience.

What do you get out of this? You get to be in control, for one thing. You set the stage and arrange every moment of the action. For another, you release your own inhibitions that may have held you back from complete sexual satisfaction. You find that stimulating your partner is a bigger turn-on that you ever thought possible. Finally, you dump any negative attitude you may have had about sex when you focus on the moment.

Virgo on the Twelfth-House Cusp

Your imagination works overtime when you are planning a sexual encounter. If you allow yourself to be influenced too easily, there is no planning, and therefore no dynamic tension to increase the level of pleasure. Your attention to the details of the physical environment makes a huge difference. The setting doesn't have to be opulent to please you. In fact, you prefer crisp sheets, functional attire, and other practical preparations, like a bath.

Because you are a receptive soul, you have researched what your partner really likes. You are willing to add frilly, silly, or even chilly (yes, ice) components to your otherwise neat and tidy sexual setting. Even though this means creating a look or feel that goes beyond what you personally want, you are able to look past the additions and see their effect on your partner..

Libra on the Twelfth-House Cusp

Your secret wish is that love and sex could be the most beautiful, harmonious experiences of your life. Sometimes the reality doesn't come close. You occasionally try some rather questionable postures or partners just to see what it is like. Later you see it was a good thing that you created utmost privacy for these forays into sexual experimentation. The sheer lack of tastefulness would embarrass you if it became public!

On the positive side, you are able to refine your bedroom for the most passionate, ecstatic acts of physical love. You make sure everything is on hand. You provide a meal or snacks to fuel the flames. You warm the bath towels in the winter and provide cooling drinks in the summer. Most of all, when the plan is ready, you bring a carefree outlook to the bedroom and shut out all your worries and cares.

Scorpio on the Twelfth-House Cusp

You spend time working in secret, pursuing metaphysical interests. All the while you accumulate ideas for enhancing your sex life. You may have tried satisfying yourself. This is helpful, as it helps you learn what will increase your satisfaction with your partner. You consider sexual acts that many people would never dream of, let alone try. You consider them, but you don't have to follow through.

You are easily tempted. A glance at a likely partner may be all you need to get into the mood. Straying from your mate for a one-night stand or extended affair is certainly possible. You sometimes believe you could have any partner you desire. You have to demonstrate that you can resist temptation if you want to earn your partner's trust. You may choose to live in relative seclusion.

Sagittarius on the Twelfth-House Cusp

You like solitude. You can be happy living a quiet life out of the mainstream of social activity. You certainly pursue your sex life in privacy. Your friends might be surprised to know just how important sex is to you. They certainly see very little of that side of your personality. Your partner, however, is another story.

With your partner you are able to enjoy passionate moments on a regular basis—some would say too frequently! Once you have the right partner, you are willing to pull out all the stops and experiment with a bit of alcohol or drugs to enhance your performance and experience. Be careful—a little bit goes a long way. You want to enjoy the experience, not be overwhelmed by a side effect of what you have ingested.

Capricorn on the Twelfth-House Cusp

You are modest, timid, and sometimes lonely. You may have a hard time getting into the mood for sex. You may choose to dress and undress alone. This can actually increase the mystique of sex for you and your partner. To set the mood for yourself, you must face your demons alone. You learn to take sex seriously without appearing unwilling.

You have powers of concentration that can contribute to fantastic sex. You don't lose track of what you are doing, you don't wander off into fantasyland, and you don't lose the rhythm of what you are doing. Better still, you learn from experience. Your partner will love you for remembering the intimate touches that don't matter much to you, but make all the difference in the end.

Aquarius on the Twelfth-House Cusp

You are mysterious and mystical when it comes to the private world of sex. You are in touch with the subconscious forces that drive you and your partner. You are able to pursue your own direction, and at the same time stimulate your partner along other lines. The ability to satisfy both your partner's needs and your own is central to your sense of satisfaction. It is not all about you where sex is concerned.

Because you relish the secretive quality of sex, you get the biggest thrills when you engage in activities that are somehow forbidden. It's very important to work out what is acceptable with your partner. You may try a number of things, only to decide that once was definitely enough!

Pisces on the Twelfth-House Cusp

You live in a world that has all the sexual potential you could want. You are able to ascertain your partner's deepest desire and then fulfill it. You are also able to identify your own deepest desires. Can you fulfill them by yourself? Sometimes. Other times you have to spell out what you want in practical detail. You have better results when you avoid alcohol, drugs, and cigarettes.

Your psychic talents require training. Otherwise you are open to every sexual current that swirls around you. You can exhaust yourself trying to satisfy all the sexual desires that float through your mind. And you can't satisfy them because a lot of them aren't yours and have nothing to do with what fulfills you sexually. Get the mind training you need outside the bedroom by practicing meditation and creative visualization.

15
Aspects
How Sexual Urges Are Satisfied

The aspects in your chart—the connections between the planets—indicate the natural direction in which your energies flow and the natural ways you are receptive to input from outside yourself. Planetary links indicate the flow of energy within your psyche. They also show how you connect to spiritual values. The connections between planets in your chart also indicate the most likely ways for you to connect to your sexual partner.

There are three kinds of planetary connections for you to consider where your sex life is concerned:

- Challenging connections (squares, oppositions, and conjunctions) are the most direct. The energies of both planets are in high focus. Each energy wants to shine on its own, and at the same time the two energies are coloring each other. Because one of the intentions of sexual intimacy is making this very kind of connection, challenging connections indicate how you most directly achieve intimacy. They also indicate areas where you have to put in more effort to get the favorable results you want. They sometimes show areas to avoid so that your sex life runs more smoothly. They are often "in your face" areas of life. When sexuality is involved, these connections reveal the bumpy road to love.

- Constructive connections (trines, sextiles, quintiles, and biquintiles) show ways for you to achieve intimacy more easily. They point to the creative effort you supply, the relaxed conditions where love can grow, and the opportunities that arise in your sex life.

- Some planetary connections provide special surprises in your sex life—I call these "zingers" (semisextiles, semisquares, sesquisquares, and quincunxes). They show where the greatest growth can occur, where you have to make the biggest adjustments in your thinking and feeling, and where your internal tension can enhance or detract from sexual satisfaction.

As you have already seen, each planet has its own dynamics, and therefore its connections to other planets will reflect a particular energetic style. Here's an example of how one thing can be affected in numerous ways. Suppose you want something to drink. You head for the kitchen, and you find a lot of possibilities. You could have plain water, straight from the tap. The water might be in the refrigerator, chilled just the way you like it in summer. You might use filtered or bottled water. Maybe you like green tea. Maybe you actually like water that has been sitting out for a while to reach room temperature. Maybe you don't really like plain water, so you squeeze some oranges instead. The tactile experience of squeezing the oranges may be as satisfying as the juice itself.

The ways in which we approach sexuality are multifaceted. The connections between the planets show your individual style in each area of your sex life. As you read about the aspects in your chart, you will become familiar with your compatible tendencies as well as the seemingly opposed desires you find within yourself. You can choose to highlight specific connections at different times. You will continue to learn about the variety of sexual desire and pleasure throughout your life, so don't stop with the easiest connections—plan a lifetime of exploration!

How to Make the Most of the Aspects You Have

The Sun

Aspects to the Sun indicate the channels through which sexual stimulation works best for you. Planets that connect to the Sun also connect to your deepest character traits and allow for very direct communication and expression. Here you discover how to use your willpower to enhance your sex life instead of blocking satisfaction.

The Moon

Aspects to the Moon indicate ways for you to enhance your emotional pleasure. The emphasis of Moon aspects is on expression of the feminine. Buried sexual memories can be accessed through lunar aspects.

Mercury

Mercury aspects reflect the nature of verbal and nonverbal communication that can affect your sexual response. They indicate how you use your intellectual abilities to further sexual pleasure. On the downside, they show where or how you scatter your sexual energy.

Venus

Connections to Venus point to the beauty found in sexual pleasure. Rhythm may be a factor. Basically Venus relates to love in all its manifestations. Venus aspects indicate how you attract potential partners. You can use these connections as a guide to creating the most attractive self-image possible.

Mars

Mars connections indicate the path of physical energy. They show how and where sexual energy most directly and easily flows. Hence Mars connections indicate where desires of all kinds can be satisfied. Because Mars indicates sexual function, connections with other planets define the physical nature of your sex life.

Jupiter

Jupiter reflects idealism. Sometimes Jupiter connections show extremes of sexual activity or impractical possibilities. This planet can indicate both areas of confidence and areas where we exaggerate. It can also indicate dissipation. Jupiter connections to other planets indicate the expansive/excessive quality of your sex life.

Saturn

Saturn reflects caution. Thus Saturn is often thought to be a limiting or restricting factor. Actually Saturn indicates the structure of your sex life. It shows where fear and shame can arise. It also indicates the level of sensitivity to touch, the level of endurance to be expected, and the wisdom to be developed within your sex life. Saturn connections with other planets reveal areas of deep focus.

Uranus

Uranus is the planet of surprises. Just when you think you have everything figured out, Uranus connections can reveal a whole new set of possibilities. These are the areas of unconventional sexual impulse and action. These are also areas where intuition plays a big part in your eventual sexual satisfaction. Sometimes abrupt, sometimes rebellious, Uranus connections are always interesting.

Neptune

The level of impressionability in your sex life is indicated by Neptune. On the positive side, you find psychic wisdom and immense empathy. On the downside, you find self-deception and vagueness. Neptune provides a window into your own potential for unity and imagination. It shows where fantasy can be employed in your sex life.

Pluto

Pluto connections are all about power. If power means coercion, then your sex life will have some serious problems. If power means mutual, intense, transformative experiences, then look to your Pluto connections for ways to achieve your goals. The energy can be destructive, or it can help tear down unnecessary boundaries. Pluto connections show you where paths to sensuality and spirituality are not that far apart.

Summary

As you read about the aspects in your chart, you will see how the nature of one planet affects the nature of another. The aspect itself indicates the quality of the connection, while the planets indicate the energies that form the connection. After you read about each aspect, think about how the two planets can work together to provide the best of their different natures, thereby supporting and improving sexual pleasure.

Sun Aspects

Sun/Moon Challenging Aspect

Your sex life incorporates the alignment of your spirit with your waking life. Sexuality, for you, is a matter of balance between the physical and the nonphysical realms. Your own balance lends stability to your sexual relationships.

Internal conflict manifests in your sex life as dissatisfaction, regardless of your partner's efforts to satisfy you. In addition, when your mind should be in the bedroom, you sometimes find that it is focused elsewhere. Meditation can help you develop the ability to focus on the present moment.

Sun/Mercury Challenging Aspect

Generally you express your thoughts about sexuality easily. At puberty this was probably accentuated, and may even have caused some embarrassment to you or your friends. Your opinions about sex are subjective. Does your partner agree with you? Ask to find out.

For sex to be at its best, you need to avoid alcohol, drugs, or anything else that distracts you. You need to be as clear as possible about what you are doing. Mental activity can make you nervous in bed. A relaxing massage can help.

Sun/Venus Challenging Aspect

You have strong magnetism that attracts partners with sex on their minds. You are likely to form a strong love union at some point, leaving behind any promiscuous tendencies, but still reveling in the intense pleasure of sex.

You are a seeker of pleasure. You are a capable sexual partner because you have a wide range of experience or because you bring sexual tension to each encounter, or both. You are at risk for health problems if you engage in indiscriminate sexual activity.

Sun/Mars Challenging Aspect

Your sex life and physical vitality seem to be one and the same. You want to attain the highest and best sexual ecstasy, and may be somewhat hasty in choosing a partner. Your passionate approach to life sometimes causes strain in your relationships.

You are strong and vital, but sometimes a bit too quick where sexual pleasure is concerned. You also judge yourself and your performance rather harshly. Fertility is never an issue for you. Extraordinary sexual experience is.

Sun/Jupiter Challenging Aspect

Your joyous approach to life extends to your sexual relationships. If more is better and a certain amount of greed is good, then your approach to sex is right on the money. Your creative energy gets a boost from healthy sexual activity.

You may have experienced a delay in development that caused you to lag behind your friends in sexual development. You have the capacity to become utterly absorbed when engaging in physically pleasurable activities. Ill health can occasionally prevent you from enjoying sex.

Sun/Saturn Challenging Aspect

Your sex life is somewhat inhibited by overly deliberate thinking. Karmic conditions need to be addressed to lift a sense of gloominess and doubt. Your sexual development may have been somewhat delayed.

You are a somewhat pessimistic individual. This need not prevent you from experiencing material and physical pleasure, although gloomy behavior will reduce your pleasure potential because you are busy focusing on the negative side of every experience. Sex later in life may be a lot more pleasurable for you.

Sun/Uranus Challenging Aspect

Your sexual fantasies include fireworks and dramatic music, along with rhythmic movements that all build together to an explosive climax. Ordinary partners can't live up to this expectation all the time, but when they do . . .

Rhythm plays a big part in your sexuality. This could involve the rhythm of the fertility cycle. It certainly reflects the fact that proper rhythm enhances sexual stimulation for you.

Sun/Neptune Challenging Aspect

You are so totally impressionable that sexual intimacy can be overwhelming. You are seductive, and you can be seduced. Until you learn to discriminate in your choice of sexual partners, you are open to exploitation and chaotic relationships.

You are susceptible to gloominess and self-deception. Your partner could be an angel, and you might not see it. Select your sexual partners with care, and avoid the use of any alcohol or drugs in association with your sex life.

Sun/Pluto Challenging Aspect

All of the body's regenerative processes are strong within you. You want power along with physical satisfaction. You may push ideal partners away if you demand too much too soon. Arrogance is not your best character trait where sex is concerned.

You want to be in control all the time. Sex is better when you lose control!

Sun/North Node Challenging Aspect

You love to be close to your partner. It doesn't always have to be about sex either. Other kinds of physical contact enhance your intellectual and spiritual experience, and also provide sexual intimacy.

Your associates dictate the quality of your social experience. By extension, they can also affect your sex life dramatically. Greater care in choosing a partner is essential for your well-being.

Sun/Ascendant Challenging Aspect

Your physical senses are highly tuned. This makes the physical side of sex very stimulating and, at the same time, something to inspire discrimination. Choose your partner well, and you will feel secure in a more passive role.

Whatever is on your mind affects your sexual responsiveness. Sexual satisfaction improves when you set aside angry or resentful attitudes altogether, including those not associated with your partner.

Sun/Midheaven Challenging Aspect

Unless or until you gain a high level of self-awareness, your sex life will be less than wonderful. Developing consciousness of your innermost feelings and desires is up to you. Awareness of your partner's feelings can be gained through greater self-awareness.

Throughout your life you seek personal clarity in career, in relationships, and also in your approach to sexuality. You may have sexual attitudes that demand attention, lest you lose interest in your sex life altogether. Sexuality provides opportunities for you to learn more about yourself. Conscious effort means that you have better results when you are not inebriated or using any drugs. Mental clarity enhances sexual satisfaction.

Sun/Moon Constructive Aspect

Your inner balance makes it easy for you to take advantage of sexual opportunities. Visual images stimulate your libido, so make sure the environment is pleasing for intimate encounters. Mutual satisfaction is a natural expectation for you. Work with your partner to achieve it.

Sun/Mercury Constructive Aspect

You can keep your eye—and your mind—on the prize where sexual fulfillment is concerned. You bring all your knowledge and skills to your sex life. You often find that something you learned in a different venue can be successfully applied to achieving sexual satisfaction.

Sun/Venus Constructive Aspect

Physical beauty is a huge attraction for you. You can also find the beauty within another person even when the surface attraction is not so strong. You like to create a harmonious atmosphere for sex. You have a wide range of expression in your sex life.

Sun/Mars Constructive Aspect

You are willing to fight for your sexual relationship, and you put significant effort into improving it. You are also capable of the highest sexual satisfaction. To top it off, your libido is backed by physical virility almost all the time.

Sun/Jupiter Constructive Aspect

Sexual satisfaction is associated with spiritual experience, and vice versa. You want your partner to share in both experiences. You subscribe to the belief that if sex is good, more is better.

Sun/Saturn Constructive Aspect

You may find that your own bed is the wrong firmness for the best sex. For example, the floor may be just the ticket when you want greater resistance. Or a tabletop. Or the bathtub, if it is big enough.

Sun/Uranus Constructive Aspect

The shared experience of your first sexual contact may be foreshadowed by disquieting dreams. It is as if the two of you do a test run on the dream plane before getting together for the physical act of love.

Sun/Neptune Constructive Aspect

Your sensitivity can leave you weak and disinterested in sex from time to time. On the other hand, the very receptivity that makes you susceptible to contagious illnesses gives you creative impressions about your sexual partner. Your psychic advantage is a steppingstone to sexual gratification, so use it to scope out the best physical stimuli.

Sun/Pluto Constructive Aspect

Physical strength is available to you for just about any sexual activity. In fact, you could support your partner as needed. Remember to use a moderate amount of force—you don't want to injure either your partner or yourself.

Sun/North Node Constructive Aspect

You are adaptable in nearly every area of your life. With very little effort, this extends to your sex life. Associations from the past give you the clues you need to decode all of your partner's desires.

Sun/Ascendant Constructive Aspect

You are able to adapt your personality to suit the sexual climate. Your self-confident approach to life is one of the reasons your sex life is satisfying. Self-esteem grows with each new experience in the sexual arena. Try not to let your ego get out of hand.

Sun/Midheaven Constructive Aspect

Mental clarity enhances sexual satisfaction. Sexuality provides opportunities for you to learn more about yourself. Conscious effort means that you have better results when you are not inebriated or using any drugs.

Sun/Moon Zinger Aspect

A direct mind-to-mind connection with your sexual partner is possible. Wow! With both mental and physical connections, you experience new heights of pleasure. Misunderstandings in the relationship come from within yourself. To solve this problem, practice meditation to heighten your mental focus.

Sun/Mercury Zinger Aspect

At puberty, a subject you were studying triggered sexual impulses. Later on, a simple mention of the subject can cause sexual arousal. These impulses have very little to do with sexual fulfillment, but are nonetheless tied in with your sexual urges.

Sun/Venus Zinger Aspect

You idealize sex and love. Sometimes you are a bit disappointed in what you get from a sexual relationship. Generally you are willing to accept the deepening feelings along with the irritations. You attract partners easily—maybe too easily.

Sun/Mars Zinger Aspect

Muscular tension enhances sexual pleasure for you. You may want to set up the environment so you can put stress on one muscle group while maintaining complete stillness in the hips and thighs. For example, the tension of keeping your hips and thighs immobile can be a real turn-on. Of course, your partner has to take the active lead for this to work.

Sun/Jupiter Zinger Aspect

Joy runs freely in your veins, and you are more than willing to share it with your partner. You are also willing to expand the sphere of your sexual experience to include philosophical and spiritual content—but mainly to increase physical pleasure.

Sun/Saturn Zinger Aspect

You may want to maintain unusual postures to enhance sexual pleasure. Hatha yoga builds the strength and balance you need for this.

Sun/Uranus Zinger Aspect

The greater your physical flexibility and endurance, the better the sex. You may want to take up kundalini yoga to develop both.

Sun/Neptune Zinger Aspect

Mystical practices work far better than any drug to enhance your sex life. For example, kundalini yoga asanas strengthen pelvic muscles, while stimulating the flow of energy throughout the body. Going deeply into the interior of your mind works!

Sun/Pluto Zinger Aspect

You want to be on top in every activity, and sex is no exception. Yet you find that the most ecstatic sexual experiences result from total surrender.

Sun/North Node Zinger Aspect

Your capacity for teamwork could lead to sex with multiple partners or fantasies about group sex.

Sun/Ascendant Zinger Aspect

Whatever is on your mind affects your sexual responsiveness. Your partner can therefore steer your sexual response in some weird directions by talking about bondage or reminding you of scenes in movies.

Sun/Midheaven Zinger Aspect

Take a risk, and learn something about yourself. Sexual intimacy provides a unique forum for exploring attitudes that developed in childhood.

Moon Aspects

Moon/Mercury Challenging Aspect

Examine the contrast between your thoughts and feelings about sex in general and about your partner in particular. You enjoy the lightest touch. Feather boa, anyone? Never lie to your sexual partner, and never gossip about your sexual exploits. Yes, never *is* a long time.

Moon/Venus Challenging Aspect

You seek love in all the wrong places, and some of the right ones. Develop evaluation skills to help you identify more appropriate romantic partners before you begin a sexual relationship.

Moon/Mars Challenging Aspect

Your excitability can lead to great quickies, but not much of a sustained effort. Use your natural emotional tension to gain greater endurance.

Moon/Jupiter Challenging Aspect

You sometimes seem indifferent to your partner—bad plan. Work out your inner sexual conflicts on your own time.

Moon/Saturn Challenging Aspect

You tend to be uncommunicative about your feelings and desires. This could be because you feel somewhat inferior. Figure out how the inferiority thing works, aside from sex. Then your sexual experience will improve, along with your sense of humor.

Moon/Uranus Challenging Aspect

Willful behavior makes your sexual experience one-sided. You also tend to exaggerate your emotional response unnecessarily. An intuitive response would work better for you and for your partner.

Moon/Neptune Challenging Aspect

The subconscious plays a big role in your fantasy life, and therefore in successful physical encounters. Allow your mind to run wild as you create a wildly passionate setting.

Incorporate details from what you know about your partner. A favorite essential oil scent can work sexual wonders.

Moon/Pluto Challenging Aspect

Your impulsive actions derail sexual relationships by causing adverse emotional reactions from your partner. Your emotional outbursts may have nothing to do with sex at all. Discover the cause—maybe repressed memories—and you will eliminate a huge impediment in your sex life.

Moon/North Node Challenging Aspect

You begin life lacking in flexibility. As you improve physical flexibility through yoga or other exercise, you will also increase emotional and intellectual adaptability, thereby improving your sexual relationship with your partner.

Moon/Ascendant Challenging Aspect

Other people get on your nerves. You are terribly sensitive to disagreements and try hard to please others. A female could help you learn to be more tolerant.

Moon/Midheaven Challenging Aspect

You sexual objectives demand investigation. They may be inconsistent with other desires. An abnormal sex drive could prevent you from fulfilling important desires in other areas.

Moon/Mercury Constructive Aspect

Your thoughtfulness is a big asset in your sex life. You tend to be a bit protective, but kindness generally enhances sexual energy for you.

Moon/Venus Constructive Aspect

Love and tenderness come naturally to you. You have an artistic flair when arranging a special tryst. Why not apply the same effort to your everyday sexual experience? The effort will pay big rewards. You benefit from the study and understanding of the female hormonal and sexual cycles.

Moon/Mars Constructive Aspect

Your willpower is backed by a huge reserve of feeling. Your openness and honesty are big assets in your sex life, so bring them with you to the bedroom. You act on your feelings, a big asset where sex is concerned.

Moon/Jupiter Constructive Aspect

On the one hand, you think more is better where sex is concerned. On the other hand, you benefit from a more commonsense approach. You eventually choose to balance quality and quantity in your sex life.

Moon/Saturn Constructive Aspect

Your emotional control is a sexual asset. It contributes to sustained sexual activity—you can wait for your partner. Your attention to detail is an asset as long as you focus on your partner, and not on side issues.

Moon/Uranus Constructive Aspect

Your emotions run deep. Sometimes you are astonished by the ideas that emerge while in the throes of sexual passion. You have radical ideas about how to enhance physical pleasure. If you occasionally overdo things, give your body a rest before trying again.

Moon/Neptune Constructive Aspect

You have intensely vivid dreams that supply images and actions to excite your sex life. The actual experience is different from your dreams because (1) your sex partner is a real, living person, and (2) dream experiences are idealized (or demonized) in ways that escape us in waking life. Use your imagination to add a mystical, exotic touch to your bedroom.

Moon/Pluto Constructive Aspect

You have deep channels of emotional passion. To reach the depths and heights of physical passion, your best bet is to pursue sexual experiences with one partner over an extended period of time. Only in this way can you develop the trust necessary to open your emotional pathways.

Moon/North Node Constructive Aspect

Through involvement with women, you learn about subtle details of sensuality. If you haven't paid attention in the past, you may have to live with some women to get the full range of information—even if you are female!

Moon/Ascendant Constructive Aspect

You are willing to adapt to circumstances and to the desires of your partner. Women can teach you a lot about improving your sexual experience. Try their way, and then decide for yourself.

Moon/Midheaven Constructive Aspect

Your spiritual values are profoundly important to you. When you think of sex as part of your spiritual life and make spiritual practice a prelude to your sex life, you enhance physical pleasure. Create peace, and you will enrich both your spiritual awareness and your physical pleasure.

Moon/Mercury Zinger Aspect

Your nerves are profoundly sensitive. This is true on both the emotional and physical levels.

Moon/Venus Zinger Aspect

You are one of the few people who can get somewhere sexually by sharing your art collection. Be prepared to talk about each piece (of art).

Moon/Mars Zinger Aspect

Your very sensitive emotional on/off switch makes for quick engagement, and also a quick getaway.

Moon/Jupiter Zinger Aspect

The good news is that you are popular with a lot of people. The bad news is that your popularity can lead you to have more than one sexual relationship at a time. This is not fair to your partners or yourself.

Moon/Saturn Zinger Aspect

Your sense of duty comes in handy when your partner needs something out of the ordinary in the sexual arena.

Moon/Uranus Zinger Aspect

Your ability to perceive your partner's feelings helps only if you mention what you have observed. You will be perceived as a caring partner, if nothing else.

Moon/Neptune Zinger Aspect

Your psychic senses come in handy when you seek to understand your partner's needs. Yes, the same sensitivity that interferes with your own sexual experience can enhance your partner's.

Moon/Pluto Zinger Aspect

The same emotional extremes that get you in trouble with your sexual partner were a huge part of the original attraction. Therefore, retain and cultivate your emotional nature.

Moon/North Node Zinger Aspect

Living with your sexual partner is a requirement. Flings do not enhance your sexual satisfaction. Even when you are living together, it takes time for you to adapt to your partner's quirks. Allow time for the relationship to deepen. Then you get the very best sex possible.

Moon/Ascendant Zinger Aspect

You are not your emotions. At least, that's not all you are. Creative effort pays off in the sexual arena when you allow your emotions to permeate your entire persona. Think about it: you want to know when you are satisfying your partner, right? Let your partner know when you reach higher plateaus of satisfaction.

Moon/Midheaven Zinger Aspect

When your soul vibrates on your partner's wavelength, you enter a profound state of spiritual awareness. Thus it is important for you to be discriminating in your choice of partner. Any sexual encounter can touch you very deeply, so be sure each encounter will be remembered in a positive light.

Mercury Aspects

Mercury/Venus Challenging Aspect

You can be really conceited about your sexual prowess. At the same time, you are sometimes overly sensitive when it comes to sex. You want the pleasure, and you want it to come wrapped in an elegant, even luxurious package. You find that you get better results when you inject a bit of humor into your sex life.

Mercury/Mars Challenging Aspect

You like a good argument. While engaging in sexual intimacy is sometimes a good way to make up after a fight, this should not become a habit. Reserve your energy to give your sexual passion a rocket boost of energy, instead of wasting your time finding fault with your partner and tearing down the trust between you.

Mercury/Jupiter Challenging Aspect

You want more, and you want it now. Where sex is concerned this attitude can lead to a loose approach that prevents deeper intimacy and the development of a successful relationship. Remember, it's not the number of sexual relationships you have that determines your success, it's the quality you achieve.

Mercury/Saturn Challenging Aspect

Shyness or narrow-mindedness can prevent you from achieving the highest physical satisfaction. In fact, these attitudes can actually interfere with the nervous system, preventing transmittal of physical sensations. You can enhance sexuality in two ways. Cultivate longer-term relationships to overcome shyness naturally, and broaden your thinking through reading, conversations with trusted friends, and even experimentation.

Mercury/Uranus Challenging Aspect

Intuition plays a role in your sex life. Pay attention to subtle yet revealing clues about your partner. Then ask questions to explore your insights. Be truthful, but not so blunt that you cause hurt feelings.

Mercury/Neptune Challenging Aspect

Your judgment can be somewhat faulty when it comes to your selection of sexual partners. You may confuse sexual intimacy with love. They are not the same, as you will find out. You expect sincerity from your partner, and are disappointed when you discover that your partner faked love. You learn through experience to stick close to the truth in all sexual matters.

Mercury/Pluto Challenging Aspect

You are very quick on the uptake—too quick sometimes. Sexual satisfaction is about sustained contact, both physical and emotional. You need to learn patience where your sex life is concerned. Remember, fools rush in . . .

Mercury/North Node Challenging Aspect

You expect your verbal skills to count for something in the sex department. You may even believe that you can talk your partner into anything. This approach is doomed to disappoint you. You also tend to kiss and tell—another big mistake.

Mercury/Ascendant Challenging Aspect

Sex is not just about you. It's about your partner too. Your biggest challenge is to overcome the tendency to criticize your partner. You want sex to make you feel better, right? Remember that when you launch into a sexual critique of your partner. Don't sharpen your tongue in the bedroom.

Mercury/Midheaven Challenging Aspect

Sometimes you overestimate your sexual charms. It's possible that you are not as slick as you think. Examine your own behavior for hints about how to become a better partner in the sex game.

Mercury/Venus Constructive Aspect

You love the thought of love, and expect your sex life to focus on love just as much as physical pleasure. Your thinking is strongly influenced by your feelings. You probably think about sex more than most people.

Mercury/Mars Constructive Aspect

You go after what you want in life. Sex is no different from any other area of your life in this respect—you go after what you want. You are quick on the uptake, always have something to talk about, and can get in a sexy mood easily.

Mercury/Jupiter Constructive Aspect

Bring your literary interests into your sex life. Find erotic stories to read to your partner. Write sexually explicit messages, and leave them for your partner to find. Then employ common sense. It can keep you from making clumsy mistakes.

Mercury/Saturn Constructive Aspect

Try a slow, thorough approach to planning and executing romantic encounters. Allow enough time so there's no rush. Establish trust and confidence each time the two of you get together, and talk to your partner about your sexual thoughts and feelings. No hurry.

Mercury/Uranus Constructive Aspect

Intuition tells you how an idea is likely to pan out in the future. Where sex is concerned, it's important to validate your impressions by suggesting innovations, and listening to your partner's response. Taking this path can prevent an unfortunate miss and lead to profound spiritual experiences.

Mercury/Neptune Constructive Aspect

You enhance your sexual experience when you allow yourself to go deep within the imaginative sphere. You probably see fireworks when the sex is great. You identify subtle connections with your partner, and anchor them with a touch or a word.

Mercury/Pluto Constructive Aspect

You talk a great line where sex is concerned, and you back it up with action. You can assess the mood of an entire room of people or your own partner in a heartbeat. You can be crafty or diplomatic about sex. You may write about sex for a living.

Mercury/North Node Constructive Aspect

Your social skills make you a great party planner. Focus these talents on planning private parties for two, and you have the makings of the complete sensual experience. Dinner (or treats) and conversation are never wasted. Sharing on the intellectual level can enhance physical pleasure.

Mercury/Ascendant Constructive Aspect

You generally understand your own attitudes about sex, and you like to compare your thinking to that of your partner. You like to know a lot about a potential partner before you hop in the sack.

Mercury/Midheaven Constructive Aspect

Reflecting on previous physical encounters can be useful, but only if it is reflection, and not obsession. As you mentally log your successes, you build a base for future sexual success. Remember, it works well to tell your partner what you want, just as it helps when you ask what he or she needs.

Mercury/Venus Zinger Aspect

You have a keen sense of form, and therefore "design" your sex life artistically. There is a lighthearted quality to your passion.

Mercury/Mars Zinger Aspect

You tend to think about sex too much (if that's possible). Your expectations may not be within the capacity of any human partner to fulfill.

Mercury/Jupiter Zinger Aspect

You cause mischief for your partner, and distract from climactic sex in the bargain. Of course if your partner matches you trick for trick . . .

Mercury/Saturn Zinger Aspect

Logic and order are not the stuff of great sex. They do, however, provide the foundation. Prepare carefully, and then devote yourself totally to sexual activities.

Mercury/Uranus Zinger Aspect

You can be really tactless! You can also confuse your partner with your eccentric ideas and strange suggestions. Try offering your suggestion ahead of time to reduce the element of surprise.

Mercury/Neptune Zinger Aspect

Fantasies can come true—you have to find a way to share them first.

Mercury/Pluto Zinger Aspect

You get into and out of relationships very quickly. The same goes for getting into and out of bed. Harness your powers of suggestion. Plan sexual encounters, and adjust the plan to suit your partner's needs and desires of the moment.

Mercury/North Node Zinger Aspect

Sex can't always be about balance. Sometimes you have to take a strong lead. Develop muscular control for greater satisfaction.

Mercury/Ascendant Zinger Aspect

You are sharply attuned to any signals coming through your sense organs. Adjust every area of sensual input to enhance sexual pleasure. Check with your partner to discover different tastes in music, scent, food, and touch to enhance your pleasure. Your favorite dancing music may not work in bed.

Mercury/Midheaven Zinger Aspect

Just as your thinking can distract you in an intimate moment, so can your physical desire lead you to experiment with some very uncomfortable postures. Learn to be fully present with your sexual partner.

Venus Aspects

Venus/Mars Challenging Aspect

You have a strongly sensual nature. You are just about always interested in physical pleasure of some kind, so sexuality is high on your list of activities to engage in. Sexual maturity may come early for you, or you may have relationships relatively early in your life that revolve solely around sex.

Venus/Jupiter Challenging Aspect

There is a little voice inside you, urging you to engage in an illicit affair or to do something sexually naughty. Yet loyalty and trust are also central to your intimate partnership. Don't roam. Sexual satisfaction is a direct result of decorum and good taste. This means you should have sex only with partners who meet your high standards.

Venus/Saturn Challenging Aspect

You tend to suppress your emotions, and this leaves you unsatisfied with your sex life. Or you allow your sexual urges to take you in unhealthy directions. These tendencies may stem from your relationship with your mother or other female authority figures from childhood. To break free from the past, cultivate the ability to be in the present moment, not the past.

Venus/Uranus Challenging Aspect

Love is easily aroused. You are ready and willing to satisfy your sexual urges. You may choose to be circumspect in your choice of partners despite your readiness, as you know that not all relationships last. But then, not all sexual intimacy is reserved for long-term relationships either.

Venus/Neptune Challenging Aspect

You can mistake kindness or other attention for love. If you dress to attract people on the physical (sexual) level, you may not be attracting the type of person who can provide a lasting commitment. You can be seduced too. Take a page from the "what you see is what you get" book, and dress yourself to attract the kind of mate you most desire.

Venus/Pluto Challenging Aspect

You have fanatical tendencies where sex is concerned. You fall wildly in love, and you fall out of love again just as easily. You recognize your compulsiveness about romantic partnerships and must curb your desire to control your partner utterly.

Venus/North Node Challenging Aspect

You are generally pleasant to everyone you meet. This good-natured approach can be mistaken for a deeper sense of caring at times. You will have at least one profound love relationship in your life, one in which you and your partner adapt to each other's physical and emotional needs very successfully.

Venus/Ascendant Challenging Aspect

Love affairs are your stock in trade. You are physically attractive. Women around you contribute to your sense of beauty. Sometimes you are strongly attracted to wasteful, indulgent people who only seek pleasure and not a lasting relationship. In your youth you imagined that you had all the time in the world to achieve your goals and endless potential to achieve ultimate physical satisfaction. At some point you discover your energy is not limitless and that some indulgences are a sheer waste of time.

Venus/Midheaven Challenging Aspect

You are in love with love, and you know it. You crave the deep, intimate pleasure that comes from long-term, committed relationships. You also love the moment of falling in love. You are able to use meditation or other mental control skills to regulate your glandular systems. Thus you learn to moderate your sexual impulses. Be open to loving another person. Too much self-love makes you unattractive.

Venus/Mars Constructive Aspect

Your sexual impulse is very strong. You like passionate love and relish the touch of your bodies as you engage in physical sex. You may have reached sexual maturity or had your first sexual experience earlier than your peers. You can have sex just for sex's sake without needing long-term love to make it all work.

Venus/Jupiter Constructive Aspect

You relish the joy found in the sexual experience. You fall in love easily—perhaps too easily. You may be tempted to enter into more than one relationship at a time, causing conflict among the parties involved. Generally, you are willing to grasp sexual opportunities when they arise. You need to consider the consequences.

Venus/Saturn Constructive Aspect

You have a sense of reality that makes you cautious in the love department. You tend to be faithful to one partner and respond to an inner sense of duty. You may be attracted to someone much older, and you expect that person to be sexually experienced.

Venus/Uranus Constructive Aspect

Your sex meter is very sensitive. You get an electromagnetic charge when a potential partner walks into the room. You can be sentimental about relationships, eccentric in your choice of partners, and wildly adventurous where your sex life is concerned.

Venus/Neptune Constructive Aspect

Your erotic imagination plays a huge role in your sex life. You revel in love and expect to be carried away with physical desire. Your high ideals can become confused with your physical desires, leaving you wondering what went wrong when your partner suddenly fades out of your life.

Venus/Pluto Constructive Aspect

You want the physical side of sex first. Leave the mushy stuff for later! Your magnetism works to attract potential partners, with whom you imagine—and experience—intense pleasure. You are always madly in love with the one you're with—while you're together.

Venus/North Node Constructive Aspect

You are superadaptable. You are a good life mate because you consider your partner in everything. You love the feeling of falling in love—it makes you feel alive and strong. You are attracted to artistic or stylish partners.

Venus/Ascendant Constructive Aspect

Environment plays a huge role in your sex life. You are drawn to artistic sites and may design your own love nest around a particular theme. Then you can bring your lover home with you and begin an affair, short or long term, in your "perfect" setting.

Venus/Midheaven Constructive Aspect

You appreciate the value of a love relationship that begins with the magical infatuation of fairy tales, but then transitions into a profound love. For you, sex is best when it has a beautiful quality to it. You're not the "rip off the clothes" type.

Venus/Mars Zinger Aspect

You are stunned by the occasional switch from the heat of passion to a sudden cooling of ardor, and vice versa.

Venus/Jupiter Zinger Aspect

Adopting a happy attitude may lead to actual happiness. Pretending to be satisfied sexually doesn't work so well.

Venus/Saturn Zinger Aspect

Duty can become pleasure. Real pleasure is rarely a duty, except to yourself.

Venus/Uranus Zinger Aspect

Love is easily aroused within you, and you are ready and willing to satisfy your sexual urges—with any partner you meet. However, one day you will be permanently hooked.

Venus/Neptune Zinger Aspect

Just because you are interested in erotic art, don't think your partner wants to be filmed or photographed in the act. Sex is performance art for two.

Venus/Pluto Zinger Aspect

Spiritual transformation can emerge from intense sexual experience. Drop your compulsions to intensify the physical experience.

Venus/North Node Zinger Aspect

You have to be in love to experience great passion. Always be willing to go more than halfway.

Venus/Ascendant Zinger Aspect

Right when you are trying your hardest to be attractive to your partner, you discover you have attracted everyone else in the bargain.

Venus/Midheaven Zinger Aspect

When you catch yourself acting conceited, and you will, redirect your attention to your partner. Results prove the value of this tactic.

Mars Aspects

Mars/Jupiter Challenging Aspect

You bend the rules when your willpower gets the best of you. In sex this could mean pushing the envelope and experimenting, or it could mean bragging about your exploits. When you act without thinking, you risk hurting your partner physically or emotionally, and neither of these is a good outcome.

Mars/Saturn Challenging Aspect

Life is not all about business! Your sexual approach can be a bit harsh if you bring your businesslike style to the bedroom. You tend to accept a sexual challenge, and when you have prevailed, you lose interest. This doesn't bode well for long-term relationships. You will want to develop emotional endurance that matches your physical stamina.

Mars/Uranus Challenging Aspect

You like to argue. Sometimes you push the argument too far and contradict your partner just for the sake of the fight. This attitude is not conducive to love and respect, two requisites for a trusting relationship. You have to learn how to surrender if you are to achieve physical fulfillment through sex. You can practice by at least compromising when you and your partner disagree.

Mars/Neptune Challenging Aspect

You have great imagination, but may lack the wherewithal to take action. You also may abuse your own body through drugs or extreme sexual activities. To have a fulfilling sex life, take a giant step back from physical excess, and channel your mental energy into higher aspirations. Physical ecstasy will follow.

Mars/Pluto Challenging Aspect

You easily overwhelm your partner on the physical and emotional levels. The best sex is found when you are gentler, so shift gears! Only the very occasional partner will enjoy the kind of brutal sex you are capable of delivering. Limit that superhuman effort for isolated lifesaving moments.

Mars/North Node Challenging Aspect

You are not a natural collaborator. You have to learn how to respond consciously to your partner's sexual advances and needs, instead of reacting unconsciously. Learn to play with sex.

Mars/Ascendant Challenging Aspect

In many areas of your life you make forward progress through sheer force of will and strength. This tendency is best left outside the bedroom, as physical violence rarely enhances sexual pleasure. Just a hint of violence can be titillating.

Mars/Midheaven Challenging Aspect

You are very excitable. When under emotional stress, your actions are rather unpredictable. When your sex life is predictable, your partner will trust you more. Therefore, you need to bring your full conscious awareness to sexual intimacy, avoiding drugs or anything else that distracts you or aggravates your impulsiveness.

Mars/Jupiter Constructive Aspect

You have immense willpower to apply to business propositions. You desire freedom. You have many opportunities to direct your energy into specific activities. Sometimes you miss romantic relationships because you are too busy pursuing other interests.

Mars/Saturn Constructive Aspect

It's all about endurance. You pride yourself on being able to go as many rounds as any of your friends. You can beat yourself up a bit in the process, so take time out to relax and enjoy the atmosphere. Sometimes you resist the sexual urge in favor of a good business opportunity.

Mars/Uranus Constructive Aspect

When you focus on physical pleasure, you have nearly inexhaustible reserves of energy. Yet you appreciate the rhythm of sexual excitement and acknowledge your partner's and your own limits. Use your creative skills to develop the openness and trust necessary for complete surrender.

Mars/Neptune Constructive Aspect

Sex is best when you are inspired by imaginative stories or artistic style. It's easy for you to feel less than perfect in looks or sexual magnetism. You value a partner who always makes you feel like you are the only one, ever. Insist on safe sex.

Mars/Pluto Constructive Aspect

You can be brutal where sex is concerned. What seems like reasonable force to you could actually injure your partner, so tone it down just enough to make it fun for both of you. Less effort can result in greater satisfaction for both of you.

Mars/North Node Constructive Aspect

Sex is a collaborative effort. When both you and your partner apply yourselves to the moment, you can achieve heights of ecstasy. You can also have worthwhile partnerships that are based purely on the physical satisfaction of sex, with no thought of love.

Mars/Ascendant Constructive Aspect

You often have to get your own way where sexual encounters are concerned. You push your partner hard, and need to soft-pedal your desires a bit. Sex with colleagues? This may not be the best plan. Think of sex as a sport where you both win.

Mars/Midheaven Constructive Aspect

You learn a lot about yourself with each relationship. It can take a while to learn what turns you on the most. You are ready for sex at just about any time. Discrimination in partners will prevent the need to run away from someone you have outgrown.

Mars/Jupiter Zinger Aspect

More is always better, right? Wrong! Less frequency with more energy can lead to more profound ecstasy.

Mars/Saturn Zinger Aspect

Your intense energy is sometimes expressed through physical violence and emotional outbursts. Willful behavior meets resistance. Become familiar with your destructive side, as familiarity is the only way for you to establish self-control.

Mars/Uranus Zinger Aspect

A slightly altered sexual rhythm can overcome resistance and relieve pain. Experiment with this idea.

Mars/Neptune Zinger Aspect

You know what you want. Get up the nerve and ask your partner to try it!

Mars/Pluto Zinger Aspect

You may enjoy sexual stimulation with inanimate objects. Caution recommended.

Mars/North Node Zinger Aspect

You occasionally find yourself on the astral plane during sex. What an experience!

Mars/Ascendant Zinger Aspect

Movie chase scenes provide the images and sounds to stimulate you sexually.

Mars/Midheaven Zinger Aspect

Sexual intimacy is not all about you. Use your creative abilities to make it all about the two of you becoming an expression of unity.

Jupiter Aspects

Jupiter/Saturn Challenging Aspect

You need to develop confidence in the sexual arena, much as you have done in schooling and career. Each difficulty you encounter goes into the melting pot to become a deep pool of emotional and practical resources. This means that your sex life improves over time, and that your happiest years may come after long experience.

Jupiter/Uranus Challenging Aspect

You want freedom more than you want satisfying sex, or at least that's how it is in the beginning. As you learn to relinquish total independence in favor of a valuable emotional relationship, you find that you reach a new level of sexual satisfaction. You have a natural sense of rhythm that can become a significant factor in prolonged sexual satisfaction.

Jupiter/Neptune Challenging Aspect

You can be seduced into participating in sexual activities that are not in your best interests. You think they sound like fun, but later you have to pay a steep price. Therefore you need to create a firm sense of reality to take with you in your search for a sexual partner or a life partner. You also need to say what you really mean, and not what is convenient at the moment.

Jupiter/Pluto Challenging Aspect

You may have fanatical sexual desires that cannot be satisfied by any normal partner. You may want to conquer many sexual partners, but in doing so you will never experience the ecstasy that comes with surrender to your passions. Avoid any promiscuous activities that could get you into trouble with the authorities.

Jupiter/North Node Challenging Aspect

You tend to focus on yourself and your desires first. You seem magnanimous, but may never get around to fully considering your partner's desires and needs. In any relationship this self-centered attitude is a detriment. An agreeable demeanor will serve you better in sexual matters.

Jupiter/Ascendant Challenging Aspect

You want to feel important, and you expect your sexual partner to put you on some sort of pedestal. At the same time, you waste your sexual energies, and rarely experience the joy that is possible in a serious relationship, unless—and this is a big unless—you see your sexual relationship as a partnership in which both individuals reach higher levels of physical satisfaction and emotional contentment.

Jupiter/Midheaven Challenging Aspect

You focus a lot of energy on improving your social position, and may neglect your sexual partner in the process. A major lifestyle change, whether it be for better or worse, could endanger your intimate relationship—unless you make a special effort to consider your partner.

Jupiter/Saturn Constructive Aspect

All work and no play makes you a dull person. Therefore, schedule time for sexual games the same way you plan for appointments at work—keep the goal in mind as you plan the event. Although you have a duty to your partner, sex doesn't have to be a chore.

Jupiter/Uranus Constructive Aspect

Sex can be blissful when you allow your feelings to flow freely. You aspire to an inner ecstatic burst of joy. You are fortunate to find partners who share that desire. You are quick to grasp your partner's mood, and capitalize on it.

Jupiter/Neptune Constructive Aspect

Your depth of emotional expression will captivate your partner. Sex can be as idealized as you want, accomplished seemingly without effort. You love people in general. Focus your love on your sexual partner, and you will gain the Sun, Moon, and stars!

Jupiter/Pluto Constructive Aspect

The fact is that you want power. Where sex is concerned, you and your partner work together to raise your pleasure to the nth degree. Work separately, and you will only cause uncomfortable friction. And don't waste golden opportunities for powerful sex.

Jupiter/North Node Constructive Aspect

You seek harmony in your relationships. Where sex is concerned, this means easing into new techniques, testing the waters as you go and always stopping short of actual pain.

Marriage is important to you and so is sexual pleasure, so choose your long-term partner carefully.

Jupiter/Ascendant Constructive Aspect

You bring a positive attitude to your sexual encounters. You always seek the best from any partner. You are a team player, and expect that from your partner. Some of your best sexual experiences will occur in luxurious settings where you have few or no responsibilities except to enjoy yourselves.

Jupiter/Midheaven Constructive Aspect

You are comfortable with success in your life and expect your sex life to provide contentment. Not the wild stuff of your dreams? Perhaps not. Yet over time, you and your partner can rise to exalted heights of spiritual communion that, when paired with physical sex, is truly inspiring.

Jupiter/Saturn Zinger Aspect

Use creative techniques to build sexual tension. The resulting explosion is worth the extra effort.

Jupiter/Uranus Zinger Aspect

Be careful what you eat before sex. Your intestines can betray you.

Jupiter/Neptune Zinger Aspect

Visions may manifest while you are engaged in sexual intimacy. What a distraction!

Jupiter/Pluto Zinger Aspect

When in the throes of great sex, don't discount the possibility that you just felt a real earthquake!

Jupiter/North Node Zinger Aspect

Sexual activity can stimulate the rise of kundalini energy. Expect a rush.

Jupiter/Ascendant Zinger Aspect

Try acting out a sex-for-pay scenario. It can be titillating!

Jupiter/Midheaven Zinger Aspect

Focus on the goal, which is sexual satisfaction. Philosophize later.

Saturn Aspects

Saturn/Uranus Challenging Aspect

You tend to get into difficult sexual situations. The emotional strain prevents you from enjoying your sexual relationship. You then rebel, causing a rift with your partner that may be difficult to overcome. Illness or an accident could have a dramatic effect on your sex life at some point.

Saturn/Neptune Challenging Aspect

Don't mess around with drugs, prescription or other kinds. You have enough trouble maintaining clarity about your physical, emotional, and spiritual urges. Distrust can keep you from fully engaging in sexual intimacy. With time, you can learn the art of meaningful self-sacrifice.

Saturn/Pluto Challenging Aspect

You can be cold, severe, and even violent. None of this has a place in a sexual relationship, which by definition is built upon tenderness and trust. If you pursue your own ego needs to the detriment of those of your partner, you risk losing the very person who can provide you with the greatest sexual satisfaction.

Saturn/North Node Challenging Aspect

You don't start out on the path of adaptability. It's always your way or the highway. As you come to understand relationships with your elders better, your sexual relationships will take a positive turn. This is because you learn more about teamwork, and feel less isolated.

Saturn/Ascendant Challenging Aspect

You become depressed easily. Sexual activity can help alleviate this problem, yet your inhibited personality can leave you feeling alone, even when you are with your partner. Develop a special environment in which you always focus only on interacting with your partner. Work with your partner—share the responsibility for maintaining this intimate space.

Saturn/Midheaven Challenging Aspect

You may not be willing to work at maintaining a powerful sexual relationship. Perhaps life has caused you to lose courage, or perhaps you have been made to feel inferior in past sexual relationships. Try taking a relationship one day, one step at a time. Less is more in the pressure department.

Saturn/Uranus Constructive Aspect

The physical tension you sometimes experience can be channeled into heightened desire, and therefore greater ecstasy. If the two of you are not in sync, take some time for a massage, or simply enjoy being close enough to enjoy each other's touch.

Saturn/Neptune Constructive Aspect

Your capacity for renunciation can actually come in handy where sex is concerned. If you want to become celibate, it's possible. If you want to improve your sex life, you can do that too. Give plenty of attention to your partner's needs, and be totally focused in the moment.

Saturn/Pluto Constructive Aspect

You have the capacity to grow spiritually throughout your life. Sex is one area where you see beyond your tendency to be overly harsh. Less force, guided by disciplined effort, can result in very satisfying long-term sexual relationships.

Saturn/North Node Constructive Aspect

You are rather inhibited around your own peer group, and may find better sexual relationships with people much older or younger than yourself. For one thing, you find that a mature partner can instruct you in the finer points of sex. For another, the element of competition is removed from the bedroom.

Saturn/Ascendant Constructive Aspect

You matured early in many ways. You learned everything you know about sex from your immediate environment. This may have been a good thing, especially if you used your natural shyness to avoid difficult situations in which you would not have felt safe.

Saturn/Midheaven Constructive Aspect

Slower to develop sexually, you had the advantage of watching the mistakes others made, and learning from them. You tend to stay in an intimate relationship well after other people would have run screaming from the building.

Saturn/Uranus Zinger Aspect

Precede sex with warm-up exercises. Yes, warm-up exercises.

Saturn/Neptune Zinger Aspect

Try laughing meditation with your sex partner, before, during, or after.

Saturn/Pluto Zinger Aspect

Small is not bad. It's what you do with what you have that counts.

Saturn/North Node Zinger Aspect

Meditate on tantric images to relieve inhibitions. Results are better than drugs.

Saturn/Ascendant Zinger Aspect

Try a bit of bondage. Just a bit.

Uranus Aspects

Uranus/Neptune Challenging Aspect

The emotional and physical charge of sexual intimacy can actually cause you to leave your body. However, as you cultivate the ability to stay with the intense feelings, you can achieve greater heights of ecstasy than you ever imagined possible.

Uranus/Pluto Challenging Aspect

Don't be impatient with sex. Good things take time. Focus your feelings and thoughts and stay in the present moment, and you will have a lot more fun. So will your partner. Avoid any physically risky sexual activities.

Uranus/North Node Challenging Aspect

Your intuition gets you in trouble when you act on it without testing it empirically. This means asking your partner before you try some off-the-wall sexual activity.

Uranus/Ascendant Challenging Aspect

Your emotional ups and downs can be very upsetting to your partner. In fact, they can be a total turnoff. Whenever possible, try to respond to your partner, and not to some wild emotion or impression.

Uranus/Midheaven Challenging Aspect

You tend to act first and think later. Any sexual activity outside your primary relationship could cause the loss of your partner's confidence and respect. Use your assertive powers to provide stability in your sex life. You could use some stability.

Uranus/Neptune Constructive Aspect

For you, the psychic thrill comes before the physical contact. If your foreplay is working, you shoot all the way to the stars! When you come back down, you may bring with you some unique insights into human problems and the condition of the planet.

Uranus/Pluto Constructive Aspect

Sex can transform your life. The creative energy generated by good sex can be applied to your work, your home, and all your close relationships. You are willing to invest major effort to nurture your intimate relationship. Because you enjoy the newness of a relationship the most, bring sexual innovations into your long-term relationship on a regular basis.

Uranus/North Node Constructive Aspect

Your desire to share makes you a thoughtful sexual companion. You are always looking for something new and different to spice up your sex life. Just remember that your long-term partner won't appreciate infidelity. Focus your innovative ideas within your relationship.

Uranus/Ascendant Constructive Aspect

Inventive yet unstable, your personality makes for wild sex without any anchor to the rest of your life. You love moving around and meeting new partners. Bring that energy to one intimate relationship long enough to reach the profound depths of which you are definitely capable.

Uranus/Midheaven Constructive Aspect

You pursue sexual desires energetically. Sometimes this magnifies body tension and emotional stress. Your futuristic vision leaves you ready for whatever comes up, moment to moment. This is not the stuff of long-term relationships, but it sure can be fun!

Uranus/Neptune Zinger Aspect

If sexual fantasies tend to carry you away from the moment, prepare food ahead of time that you can nibble on. Eating will bring you back to the present.

Uranus/Pluto Zinger Aspect

Use inventive methods to transform your sexual relationship. Be creative!

Uranus/North Node Zinger Aspect

Dreams provide ideas for heightened sexual passion.

Uranus/Ascendant Zinger Aspect

Your nervous system steps up to the plate quickly—sometimes too quickly.

Uranus/Midheaven Zinger Aspect

Practice controlling your breathing for maximum pleasure.

Neptune Aspects

Neptune/Pluto Challenging Aspect

You can easily misinterpret signals from other people. Where sex is concerned, you must be willing to speak the words, ask the questions, and do everything possible to be clear about what each of you wants and expects from the relationship. Oh, and don't lie. Ever. About anything.

Neptune/North Node Challenging Aspect

You often feel like you don't belong. This can happen in a group or during one of those intimate sexual moments.

Neptune/Ascendant Challenging Aspect

Don't attempt to develop a sexual relationship while you are using any mind-altering substance. You will find that any drug, including caffeine or nicotine, dulls your senses and makes you do or say something stupid to harm your sexual partner.

Neptune/Midheaven Challenging Aspect

You start out with a lack of confidence in your sexual abilities. You can be led down the garden path to some extreme sexual practices. Develop greater self-awareness. When you do, you will be able to say what you want and need, and not be seduced into everything a partner suggests.

Neptune/Pluto Constructive Aspect

This aspect is shared by entire generations of people, so your partner is very likely to have it in the birth chart too. You have an interest in mystical and supernatural phenomena. This interest can enhance your sex life when you apply what you know about your inner life to your sexual partnership. You may decide to explore extraordinary sexual possibilities. You may instead come to see your sex life as a significant part of your spiritual life, and vice versa.

Neptune/North Node Constructive Aspect

You desire to live in a communal setting, and may consider multiple sexual partners. You tend to believe that people, yourself included, are capable of more openness than they are. Don't push the group encounter too hard, or you may push your partner away.

Neptune/Ascendant Constructive Aspect

Dreamy and impressionable, you love a romantic setting, soft music, and a very, very light touch. Other people find it easy to control and manipulate you, especially in your youth. You have had to open your psychic senses to others early in the game to spot sticky sexual situations and avoid them.

Neptune/Midheaven Constructive Aspect

You have imaginative, far-reaching goals that may not be attainable where physical sex is concerned. You expect too much from the typical partner. Your sex life benefits from considering the perverted side of human nature. That doesn't mean you are perverted. It means you understand your own motivations in the context of the full range of sexual possibilities. The deeper you go, the better the sex gets.

Neptune/Pluto Zinger Aspect

Create a healthy lifestyle to enhance sexual satisfaction.

Neptune/North Node Zinger Aspect

Stretching helps develop greater flexibility, which is always a sexual asset.

Neptune/Ascendant Zinger Aspect

Reveal your weaknesses occasionally. It's a refreshing change.

Neptune/Midheaven Zinger Aspect

When you meditate, take an internal survey of your body from time to time. This helps your sexual focus.

Pluto Aspects

Pluto/North Node Challenging Aspect

Your sex life will feel cramped if you don't discuss your needs and desires with your partner. Say what you are thinking, but be gentle about it.

Pluto/Ascendant Challenging Aspect

You want power and control. Where sex is concerned, this approach won't work the way you want it to, at least not in the long run.

Pluto/Midheaven Challenging Aspect

You are more willing to take chances than most people. Your sex life is not an arena for gaining public acclaim. It can be a way to transform your life, though. Support your partner, act just a bit more prudently, and then let your restraints go in the moment of sexual climax.

Pluto/North Node Constructive Aspect

Your desire to expand your group of associations may interfere with the potential for a truly satisfying sexual relationship.

Pluto/Ascendant Constructive Aspect

You are fascinating, and therefore attract sexual partners easily. If you then push too hard, you can lose them just as fast. Even if you are hot to try a new technique, restrain yourself if your partner is unwilling. As sexual excitement peaks during intimate acts, you may feel an accompanying surge of psychic energy, such as intuitive insights into the nature of life.

Pluto/Midheaven Constructive Aspect

You want to be important and successful. To do that in your sex life, focus on your partner, cultivate depth in your relationship, and at the same time retain your natural independence. That way you remain tantalizing.

Pluto/North Node Zinger Aspect

Use birth control, even after you are sure it is unnecessary. Otherwise, expect pregnancy.

Pluto/Ascendant Zinger Aspect

Mental power is fascinating. Brute physical force is a turnoff.

Pluto/Midheaven Zinger Aspect

After an illness, moderate sex can be a recuperative aid.

16
Case Study
Relating on the Sexual Plane

As you read through this book, you will begin to understand your own sexuality. You will discover things about yourself and how you respond physically and emotionally. You will become more aware of inconsistencies and outright contradictions in your own behavior in the bedroom.

You may have already prepared CD-ROM interpretations for yourself and your sexual partner. If not, this might be a good time to do so. If you have, you have certainly learned a lot about this other person, and you are aware of the differences between the two of you where sexual desires are concerned.

Not to despair! Differences are a good thing! They can present some challenges, but for the most part they add spice to a relationship. Without them, your sexual relationship might become dull and boring.

To illustrate how to use this book and the interpretations from the program, I have created interpretations for a fictional couple—I made up the birth data. The charts are, however, just like the charts of people who may have been born on these dates. The interpretations look a lot like the charts and interpretations you get from the program, combined with the relevant aspects you read about in the previous chapter.

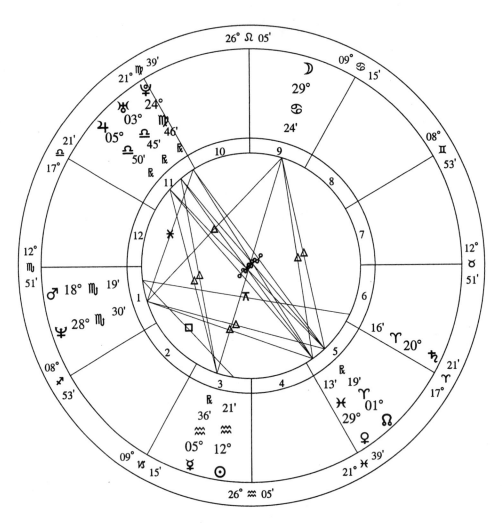

Chart 6: Aquarius Partner
February 1, 1969 / Seattle, Washington / 1:17 AM PST
Koch Houses

Aquarius Partner

Sometimes it isn't about love. Or perhaps I should say it isn't *just* about love. You have physical desires, and you want to find ways to satisfy those desires. Everyone grows up with all sorts of fantasies about the perfect lover and the perfect physical chemistry. We have come to expect these fantasies to be satisfied by the person with whom we fall in love, and it isn't always the perfect bliss we anticipated.

Astrology is able to examine every area of your life. Your sex life is no exception. Through understanding your own desires and how they fit into your fantasies, you learn how to ask your partner to meet your needs. You can also take a look at your partner's astrology chart to see what his or her fantasies and needs are all about. The two of you can create a whole new level of passion by understanding how your desires are similar—and different.

The goal of this book is to use astrology to inform you about the myriad desires, needs, and expectations people have where sexuality is concerned. You will learn that the way you were taught as a child or teen is definitely not all there is to your physical passion. You will probably find out that what you work out logically is not totally satisfying. You may even discover keys to your own pleasure that you never suspected. You will certainly learn to appreciate the differences between you and your partner, and how to play (not work) with each other's fantasies and desires.

Imagine having twelve different approaches to sexual thoughts, feelings, and expression. Then imagine having twelve different ways to implement each of those expressions. Then imagine combining your 144 varieties with those of your partner. Your sex life just improved by over 2,000 percent! Astrology can help you discover subtleties you never knew existed.

So get a glass of your favorite wine (or soda), a few snacks, and this book. Get cozy and warm, and begin your voyage of discovery as you map your sex life in all its many manifestations. Your physical pleasure will never be the same!

Your Sexual Individuality

There are multiple facets to your sexuality. That's a given. We will begin by examining your sexuality from an individual perspective. While most of us associate sexuality with a partner, in reality we each possess our own individual sexual signature.

Sun in the Air Element

You rely on your capacity to think things through. When you spend too much time thinking about your sex life, though, you find that you never get past the thought stage! Your logical mind is best used in devising a plan for your sex life. Then set logic aside and enjoy the process.

Sun in a Fixed Sign (stable)

You are a determined person. This affects your physical desires in that you keep searching for the most satisfaction you can give and receive. You like consistency, and therefore may not have your best sex in unusual circumstances. Your power reserves allow you to keep going for hours when the setting is right. You are nothing if not thorough in your exploration of physical pleasure.

Sun in Aquarius (fixed air)

You have superior powers of observation. This may not seem like a skill to use in your sex life, but think about it. You can catalog each encounter, log the successes, and rank them in some order. You have a storehouse of information about human nature that can be applied in each unique sexual encounter. You rebel against the norm, and therefore are likely to consider—and try—a wide variety of sexual activities. Through cooperation you and your partner are able to reach greater heights of physical pleasure. A tip for Aquarius' partner: your Aquarian likes to talk about sex. Do not dismiss this as a frivolous comment. You can literally talk your partner into a sensual state of bliss! This can take the pressure off where physical performance is concerned. If your partner is in the zone mentally, the physical part is icing on the cake.

Sun in the Third House

Versatility is your middle name. When one sexual technique or approach doesn't work, you try another. And another. You are willing to learn something new from your sexual partner(s), and you may experiment with multiple partners or with more than one relationship at a time. Your sexual libido fluctuates, depending largely on the information you absorb from your environment. Thus the setting has a huge impact on your sexual performance and enjoyment. Be creative and enhance the ordinary with extraordinary music, scents, or food.

Sun Conjunct Mercury

Generally you express your thoughts about sexuality easily. At puberty this was probably accentuated, and may even have caused some embarrassment to you or your friends. Your opinions about sex are subjective. Does your partner agree with you? Ask to find out.

Sun Semisquare Venus

You are a seeker of pleasure. You are a capable sexual partner because you have a wide range of experience or because you bring sexual tension to each encounter, or both. You are at risk for health problems if you engage in indiscriminate sexual activity.

Sun Square Mars

You are strong and vital, but sometimes a bit too quick where sexual pleasure is concerned. You also judge yourself and your performance rather harshly. Fertility is never an issue for you. Extraordinary sexual experience is.

Sun Trine Jupiter

You are a morally upstanding individual. This ought not prevent you from also experiencing material and physical pleasure. Arrogant behavior will reduce your pleasure potential because you are busy trying to look and act cool, when hot is more to the point. Interestingly enough, a more spiritual demeanor—one of compassion and caring—will take you to the heights of pleasure you seek.

Sun Quintile Neptune

Your sensitivity can leave you weak and disinterested in sex from time to time. On the other hand, the very receptivity that makes you susceptible to contagious illnesses gives you creative impressions about your sexual partner. Your psychic advantage is a steppingstone to sexual gratification, so use it to scope out the best physical stimuli.

Sun Sesquisquare Pluto

You want to be on top in every activity, and sex is no exception. Yet you find the most ecstatic sexual experiences result from total surrender. So learn to take turns on top for maximum satisfaction.

Sun Square Ascendant

Whatever is on your mind affects your sexual responsiveness. Sexual satisfaction improves when you set aside angry or resentful attitudes altogether, including those not associated with your partner.

So far we have explored just one of the factors in your birth chart—the Sun. Now let's look at other areas of your chart that relate to your sex life.

Physical Desires

Physical desires are be mapped by the planets Venus and Mars.

Venus in Pisces

You seek a relationship that is based upon love. If you seek only sexual pleasure, you may be sorely disappointed. You can be seduced by your lover, and you also are capable of seducing others. Your pleasant demeanor and sociability put you in the path of many potential partners. You must develop discernment if you are to avoid disappointment in intimate relationships. A tip for Venus in Pisces' partner: don't act like a mechanic. Instead, act as if each sexual encounter is a social event just for two. Pay attention to what turns your partner on one time, and remember to try it again, or even just allude to the last time.

Perhaps the most sexually attractive part of your body is your feet. You may think this odd, but extra care of the feet, along with thoughtful selection of slippers, socks, stockings, and shoes, can make a huge difference in your overall appearance. Your partner will want to look at, touch, and admire your feet, and may give you jewelry for your ankles or toes. You and your partner may find that touching your feet or touching with them is physically arousing.

Mars in Scorpio

Physical satisfaction seems like it is a live-or-die situation—you must have your physical needs met in order to feel alive. You can be ruthless in your pursuit of sexual partners, and you can turn on them just as easily if they don't meet your standards. You sometimes waste your time and energy on meaningless relationships, but you are also capable of deep and abiding passion with a single partner. A tip for Mars in Scorpio's partner: it will seem like no amount of stimulation is too much. It can be verbal or physical—both are effective.

Venus Opposite Jupiter

There is a little voice inside you, urging you to engage in an illicit affair or to do something sexually naughty. Yet loyalty and trust are also central to your intimate partnership. Don't roam. Sexual satisfaction is a direct result of decorum and good taste. This means you should have sex only with partners who meet your high standards.

Venus Opposite Uranus

Love is easily aroused. You are ready and willing to satisfy your sexual urges. You may choose to be circumspect in your choice of partners despite your readiness, as you know that not all relationships last. But then, not all sexual intimacy is reserved for long-term relationships either.

Venus Trine Neptune

Your erotic imagination plays a huge role in your sex life. You revel in love and expect to be carried away with physical desire. Your high ideals can become confused with your physical desires, leaving you wondering what went wrong when your partner suddenly fades out of your life.

Venus Opposite Pluto

You have fanatical tendencies where sex is concerned. You fall wildly in love, and you fall out of love again just as easily. You recognize your compulsiveness about romantic partnerships and must curb your desire to control your partner utterly.

Venus Conjunct North Node

You are generally pleasant to everyone you meet. This good-natured approach can be mistaken for a deeper sense of caring at times. You will have at least one profound love relationship in your life, one in which you and your partner adapt to each other's physical and emotional needs very successfully.

Venus Biquintile Midheaven

You are capable of a deeply meaningful love, and it seems you practice falling in love. As you gain experience, you learn to stick with a relationship long enough to discover what depths of physical and emotional passion are possible. You learn to create an environment appropriate for a great love. In this way satisfaction increases.

Venus Sesquisquare Ascendant

In your youth you imagined that you had all the time in the world to achieve your goals and endless potential to achieve ultimate physical satisfaction. At some point you discover your energy is not limitless and that some indulgences are a sheer waste of time.

Mars Semisquare Jupiter

You bend the rules when your willpower gets the best of you. In sex this could mean pushing the envelope and experimenting, or it could mean bragging about your exploits. When you act without thinking, you risk hurting your partner physically or emotionally, and neither of these is a good outcome.

Mars Quincunx Saturn

Your intense energy is sometimes expressed through physical violence and self-absorbed emotional outbursts. Willful behavior meets resistance. Become familiar with your destructive side, as familiarity is the only way for you to establish self-control.

Mars Semisquare Uranus

You like to argue. Sometimes you push the argument too far and contradict your partner just for the sake of the fight. This attitude is not conducive to love and respect, two requisites for a trusting relationship. You have to learn how to surrender if you are to achieve physical fulfillment through sex. You can practice by at least compromising when you and your partner disagree.

Mars Sesquisquare North Node

You are not a natural collaborator. You have to learn how to respond consciously to your partner's sexual advances and needs, instead of reacting unconsciously. Learn to play with sex.

Mars Conjunct Ascendant

In many areas of your life you make forward progress through sheer force of will and strength. This tendency is best left outside the bedroom, as physical violence rarely enhances sexual pleasure. Just a hint of violence can be titillating.

The Mental Side of Sex (Yes, There Is a Mental Side)

We are intelligent, thinking beings. We thrive in situations where we can apply our critical thinking to problems. Even in the arenas of romance and sexuality, thinking through our feelings can be helpful. Your approach to thinking about sexuality may be different from that of your partner, and it's good to understand those differences.

Mercury in Aquarius

Your progressive thinking leads you to try new things. In the sexual arena this brings variety into the picture, and variety is the spice of life. You are an enthusiastic sex partner, and you can be quite inventive.

Mercury in the Third House

You love variety and seek out new experiences. If your partner is too humdrum, you are tempted to stray. An overly casual approach sends the message that you don't really care beyond the physical act itself. In paying attention to the details, your planning for sexual encounters will have fantastic results.

Mercury Trine Jupiter

Bring your literary interests into your sex life. Find erotic stories to read to your partner. Write sexually explicit messages, and leave them for your partner to find. Then employ common sense. It can keep you from making clumsy mistakes.

Mercury Quintile Saturn

Try a slow, thorough approach to planning and executing romantic encounters. Allow enough time so there's no rush. Establish trust and confidence each time the two of you get together, and talk to your partner about your sexual thoughts and feelings. No hurry.

Mercury Trine Uranus

Intuition tells you how an idea is likely to pan out in the future. Where sex is concerned, it's important to validate your impressions by suggesting innovations, and listening to your partner's response. Taking this path can prevent an unfortunate miss and lead to profound spiritual experiences.

Mercury Sextile North Node

Your social skills make you a great party planner. Focus these talents on planning private parties for two, and you have the makings of the complete sensual experience. Dinner (or treats) and conversation are never wasted. Sharing on the intellectual level can enhance physical pleasure.

Your Emotional Needs Seen Through an Astrological Lens

Emotions play a huge role in sexuality. If you have ever been unable to engage in sex because of your emotions, you know this. By understanding the emotional differences between you and your partner, you take a giant step toward greater physical satisfaction.

Moon in Cancer

You are naturally affectionate. Your best sexual fulfillment comes after you have satisfied other sides of your nature. They say the way to a person's heart is through the stomach, and this is definitely true for you. When you are hungry, you are distracted from sexual matters. Eat first, and have sex later.

You need to arrange every facet of a romantic encounter to maximize sexual pleasure. This is because you sometimes have a hard time shutting out thoughts and impressions and focusing on the moment. You are likely to keep your love nest in a state of general readiness at all times. Remember, scents are powerful sexual stimulants. Use your favorites wisely.

Moon in the Ninth House

Your inner life is vivid and dramatic. You alternate between states of pessimism and optimism, and the state you are in has a major effect on your sexual experience. Remember that everything changes, including your mood. The right setting can quickly bring you to a sexually alert status, even if you were sure a few minutes earlier that sex was the furthest thing from your mind.

Moon Opposite Mercury

Examine the contrast between your thoughts and feelings about sex in general and about your partner in particular. You enjoy the lightest touch. Feather boa, anyone? Never lie to your sexual partner, and never gossip about your sexual exploits. Yes, never *is* a long time.

Moon Trine Venus

Love and tenderness come naturally to you. You have an artistic flair when arranging a special tryst. Why not apply the same effort to your everyday sexual experience? The effort will pay big rewards. You benefit from the study and understanding of the female hormonal and sexual cycles.

Moon Sextile Uranus

Your emotions run deep. Sometimes you are astonished by the ideas that emerge while in the throes of sexual passion. You have radical ideas about how to enhance physical pleasure. If you occasionally overdo things, give your body a rest before trying again.

Moon Trine Neptune

You have intensely vivid dreams that supply images and actions to excite your sex life. The actual experience is different from your dreams because (1) your sex partner is a real, living person, and (2) dream experiences are idealized (or demonized) in ways that escape us in waking life. Use your imagination to add a mystical, exotic touch to your bedroom.

Moon Sextile Pluto

You have deep channels of emotional passion. To reach the depths and heights of physical passion, your best bet is to pursue sexual experiences with one partner over an extended period of time. Only in this way can you develop the trust necessary to open your emotional pathways.

Moon Trine North Node

Through involvement with women, you learn about subtle details of sensuality. If you haven't paid attention in the past, you may have to live with some women to get the full range of information—even if you are female!

Moon Semisextile Midheaven

When your soul vibrates on your partner's wavelength, you enter a profound state of spiritual awareness. Thus it is important for you to be discriminating in your choice of partner. Any sexual encounter can touch you very deeply, so be sure each encounter will be remembered in a positive light.

Spiritual Ecstasy Through Physical Relationships

As you cultivate your relationship and establish a deeper connection with your partner, you will find that you achieve higher and higher levels of physical satisfaction. In addition, your spiritual connection is developing. Knowing each other spiritually enhances physical satisfaction immeasurably.

Neptune in Scorpio

Your senses tune in to subtle messages from your sexual partner. At the same time you are also receiving messages from within yourself. When you merge with your partner, you sometimes get rushes of psychic information. The metaphysical realm becomes congruent with the physical realm. Because of this strong affinity, all sexual encounters deserve conscious thought and careful choice. Be sure you want those psychic vibes from a potential partner before you get into bed.

Neptune in the First House

Your nervous system is sensitive to the lightest physical or psychic touch. Knowing this, be sure you choose sexual partners who are aware of your needs and desires, and not just caught up in personal desire. When you share a psychic connection with your partner, the physical component of sex is immeasurably enhanced for both of you. Deeper sexual pleasure generates emotional responses you don't usually associate with physical satisfaction. For example, you can experience sadness right along with immense joy.

Neptune Sextile Pluto

This aspect is shared by entire generations of people, so your partner is very likely to have it in the birth chart too. You have an interest in mystical and supernatural phenomena. This interest can enhance your sex life when you apply what you know about your inner life to your sexual partnership. You may decide to explore extraordinary sexual possibilities. You may instead come to see your sex life as a significant part of your spiritual life, and vice versa.

Neptune Trine North Node

You desire to live in a communal setting, and may consider multiple sexual partners. You tend to believe that people, yourself included, are capable of more openness than they are. Don't push the group encounter too hard, or you may push your partner away.

Neptune Square Midheaven

You start out with a lack of confidence in your sexual abilities. You can be led down the garden path to some extreme sexual practices. Develop greater self-awareness. When you do, you will be able to say what you want and need, and not be seduced into everything a partner suggests.

Self and Other in Intimate Partnership

The perception of self and other becomes blurred in sexual relationships. The desire to merge becomes all powerful, and then ebbs as the desire to be independent takes over. This ebb and flow of sexual energy makes for excitement in intimate relationships. Even if you are not actively engaging in sex, you can feel the tides of emotional attachment between you.

Ascendant in Scorpio

You flourish in steamy circumstances. Where sexuality is concerned, this does not mean hopping from bed to bed. It does mean sticking with one partner at a time and developing the relationship on every level, not just the physical. It may also mean having a plan for sexual encounters. Each time can be its own little conquest. Sex, for you, is inevitably associated with preservation of the species. You may select partners for their genetic nature as much as for love. You are intensely passionate in the bedroom and go more than halfway to ensure sexual fulfillment for your partner.

Descendant in Taurus

You seek a partner who appreciates a stable, comfortable environment. Owning your home can be a definite plus. You probably haven't associated home ownership with sexual pleasure, but think about it. Your partner can arrange the furniture and decorate to suit every sexual whim. A homey setting stimulates your passion too—as much or more than extreme luxury. While your passions run both hot and cold, you appreciate a more practical partner who takes care of the business of life. Your partner, to make you truly happy, must supply the warm, cozy, comfortable nest. Then your sexual passion can run wild in complete safety.

The Role of Self-Awareness in Sexuality

Know Thyself. This axiom has stood the test of time in every arena. Now you have information to help you understand your own sexual attitudes, desires, likes, and dislikes. As you listen to your inner urges, and communicate them to your partner, you find that the two of you are more willing partners.

Midheaven in Leo

You want to be treated like royalty. You don't mind being put on a pedestal and worshipped. However, you know that isn't the real you. You desire to lead, and to become a self-confident, generous leader. Therefore it's best if your sexual partner allows you to take the lead at least part of the time.

Your inspiration for leadership in physical intimacy comes from a deep desire to assert yourself. You may read up on different sexual techniques and devise ways to try them out with your partner. You love the element of surprise, although you don't wish to be surprised yourself. You can expend a lot of energy in the planning, only to find that the technique falls short of expectations. You're amazed when you occasionally find that your partner is simply not in the mood when you are.

Do You Have Sexual Karma?

Each of us has some karma to work out in the sexual arena. Intimate relationships help us by revealing our weaknesses and flaws, but also by showing where our greatest glory can be found. When dealing with a partner, it's important to realize that your karmas may collide, but they are not identical.

North Node in Aries

You seek strong associations in every area of your life. Sexually you want a strong, vital partner, but may be astonished when you find one. When two dominant types come together, there can be major sparks. In past lives you may have played the dominant role sexually, but it's more likely that you have experienced subjugation. Now you find that an overly aggressive partner is stimulating, but frightening at the same time. Basically you want to be in charge of your sex life, but are attracted to dominating types.

North Node in the Fifth House

You enjoy large social gatherings and may put so much effort into them that you have little reserved for the one-on-one intimate relationship afterward. Yet your sexual desire runs high. Balancing social and private relationships is an art. You can usually throw yourself into public situations easily. You may benefit from demonstrating a bit of reserve in public, and then engaging more deeply in your private sexual encounter. You and your partner can devise some truly creative settings or positions for intimacy. For example, find a place where you feel utterly safe and secure with the sun directly touching your skin. Hint: include sun block in your planning.

Conclusion

If you are reading this, you have probably gathered that I believe your sex life will benefit from the development of long-term relationships in which both partners are committed to the success of the relationship. While the initial flush of magnetic attraction and sexual passion will get you into a relationship, sustained attention and effort will raise your experience to the level of sheer ecstasy.

You have no doubt encountered contradictions in this material. These provide you with food for thought. How do you experience those contradictions in your sex life? Do they cause problems or add interest? As you and your partner explore sexuality together, you will resolve the contradictions within yourself and provide the greatest pleasure for your partner.

Taurus Partner

Sometimes it isn't about love. Or perhaps I should say it isn't *just* about love. You have physical desires, and you want to find ways to satisfy those desires. Everyone grows up with all sorts of fantasies about the perfect lover and the perfect physical chemistry. We have come to expect these fantasies to be satisfied by the person with whom we fall in love, and it isn't always the perfect bliss we anticipated.

Astrology is able to examine every area of your life. Your sex life is no exception. Through understanding your own desires and how they fit into your fantasies, you learn how to ask your partner to meet your needs. You can also take a look at your partner's astrology chart to see what his or her fantasies and needs are all about. The two of you can create a whole new level of passion by understanding how your desires are similar—and different.

The goal of this book is to use astrology to inform you about the myriad desires, needs, and expectations people have where sexuality is concerned. You will learn that the way you were taught as a child or teen is definitely not all there is to your physical passion. You will probably find out that what you work out logically is not totally satisfying. You may even discover keys to your own pleasure that you never suspected. You will certainly learn to appreciate the differences between you and your partner, and how to play (not work) with each other's fantasies and desires.

Imagine having twelve different approaches to sexual thoughts, feelings, and expression. Then imagine having twelve different ways to implement each of those expressions. Then imagine combining your 144 varieties with those of your partner. Your sex life just improved by over 2,000 percent! Astrology can help you discover subtleties you never knew existed.

So get a glass of your favorite wine (or soda), a few snacks, and this book. Get cozy and warm, and begin your voyage of discovery as you map your sex life in all its many manifestations. Your physical pleasure will never be the same!

Your Sexual Individuality

There are multiple facets to your sexuality. That's a given. We will begin by examining your sexuality from an individual perspective. While most of us associate sexuality with a partner, in reality we each possess our own individual sexual signature.

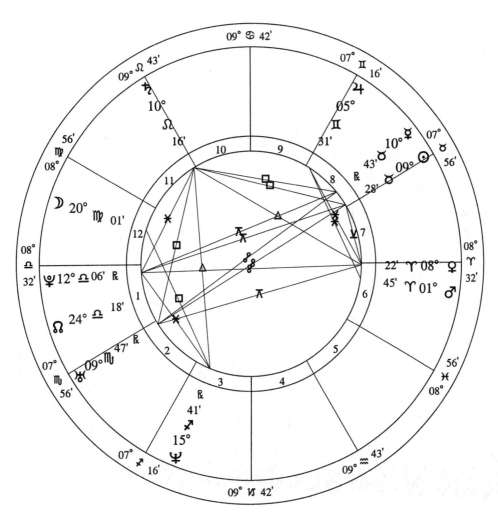

Chart 7: Taurus Partner
April 29, 1977 / St. Louis, Missouri / 5:12 PM CDT
Koch Houses

Sun in the Earth Element

You are a fundamentally practical person, and practicality extends to your perceptions about your sex life. You want a persistent partner who is willing to keep going until you are satisfied. You tend to be possessive of your partner(s) and somewhat secretive where sexuality is concerned.

Sun in a Fixed Sign (stable)

You are a determined person. This affects your physical desires in that you keep searching for the most satisfaction you can give and receive. You like consistency, and therefore may not have your best sex in unusual circumstances. Your power reserves allow you to keep going for hours when the setting is right. You are nothing if not thorough in your exploration of physical pleasure.

Sun in Taurus (fixed earth)

You bring your soul to physical passion. You also bring humor with you, and can occasionally find yourself laughing out loud when sex goes either well or badly. You love the pleasure given and received through sex. You can be jealous of your partner, sexually and in every other way as well. This emotion can dampen physical passion. You will want to work through jealous feelings on the logical level so you can set them aside. You can be selfish, which can work for you in terms of physical pleasure: the more pleasure you give to your partner, the more you are likely to receive. You are at your best when simple plans come together just the way you want. Comfort is at or very near the top of your list where sex is concerned.

Sun in the Eighth House

You have erotic dreams that pique your sexual interest. They provide a doorway from ordinary experience to the world beyond the daily grind, and you seek to open that doorway consciously through sexual activity. Massage is a good adjunct to sexual pleasure, as muscular tension detracts from your enjoyment. You focus on the external sex organs. Actual intercourse may not be as exciting as foreplay for this reason. You need to negotiate with your partner to make sure you both fulfill each other's sexual desires.

Sun Conjunct Mercury

Generally you express your thoughts about sexuality easily. At puberty this was probably accentuated, and may even have caused some embarrassment to you or your friends. Your opinions about sex are subjective. Does your partner agree with you? Ask to find out.

Sun Semisextile Venus

You idealize sex and love. Sometimes you are a bit disappointed in what you get from a sexual relationship. Generally you are willing to accept the deepening feelings along with the irritations. You attract partners easily—maybe too easily.

Sun Semisextile Jupiter

Joy runs freely in your veins, and you are more than willing to share it with your partner. You are also willing to expand the sphere of your sexual experience to include philosophical and spiritual content—but mainly to increase physical pleasure.

Sun Square Saturn

You may have experienced a delay in development that caused you to lag behind your friends in sexual development. You have the capacity to become utterly absorbed when engaging in physically pleasurable activities. Ill health can occasionally prevent you from enjoying sex.

Sun Opposite Uranus

Rhythm plays a big part in your sexuality. This could involve the rhythm of the fertility cycle. It certainly reflects the fact that proper rhythm enhances sexual stimulation for you.

Sun Biquintile Neptune

Your deep receptivity to psychic influences enhances your sex life when you use the information creatively. Use your imagination to add a mystical touch to the bedroom. You may decorate the space with imported tapestries or other objects to infuse your sex life with the exotic.

Sun Quincunx Pluto

You want to be on top in every activity, and sex is no exception. Yet you find that the most ecstatic sexual experiences result from total surrender. So learn to take turns on top for maximum satisfaction.

Sun Sextile Midheaven

Sexuality provides opportunities for you to learn more about yourself. Conscious awareness means that you have better results when you are not inebriated or using any drugs. Mental clarity, for you, enhances sexual satisfaction.

Sun Quincunx Ascendant

Whatever is on your mind affects your sexual responsiveness. Your partner can therefore steer your sexual response in some weird directions by talking about bondage or reminding you of scenes in movies.

So far we have explored just one of the factors in your birth chart—the Sun. Now let's look at other areas of your chart that relate to your sex life.

Physical Desires

Physical desires can be mapped by the planets Venus and Mars.

Venus in Aries

You are a passionate lover. You create romantic fantasies and make them come true through your creative talents. You are an adventurous lover and may cause yourself problems if you stray from your partner. You definitely believe in love at first sight.

Your head and hair are the most attractive parts of your body. Extra care and attention here can be a powerful factor in any long-term intimate relationship, and is certainly important for initial attraction of a partner. You can also use masks or makeup to focus attention. If you choose facial jewelry, be sure that it is scaled to bring out your best features. Temporary tattoos or glue-on decorations can be fun. Earrings provide infinite variety for both men and women.

Mars in Aries

You have tremendous energy. This may mean that you have sexual stamina, or it may mean that you put everything into a single encounter. Either way, your independent spirit can cause arguments that detract from your physical satisfaction.

Venus Conjunct Mars

You have a strongly sensual nature. You are just about always interested in physical pleasure of some kind, so sexuality is high on your list of activities to engage in. Sexual maturity may come early for you, or you may have relationships relatively early in your life that revolve solely around sex.

Venus Sextile Jupiter

You relish the joy found in the sexual experience. You fall in love easily—perhaps too easily. You may be tempted to enter into more than one relationship at a time, causing conflict among the parties involved. Generally, you are willing to grasp sexual opportunities when they arise. You need to consider the consequences.

Venus Trine Saturn

You have a sense of reality that makes you cautious in the love department. You tend to be faithful to one partner and respond to an inner sense of duty. You may be attracted to someone much older, and you expect that person to be sexually experienced.

Venus Quincunx Uranus

Love is easily aroused within you, and you are ready and willing to satisfy your sexual urges—with any partner you meet. However, one day you will be permanently hooked.

Venus Opposite Pluto

You have fanatical tendencies where sex is concerned. You fall wildly in love, and you fall out of love again just as easily. You recognize your compulsiveness about romantic partnerships and must curb your desire to control your partner utterly.

Venus Square Midheaven

You are in love with love, and you know it. You crave the deep, intimate pleasure that comes from long-term, committed relationships. You also love the moment of falling in love. You are able to use meditation or other mental control skills to regulate your glandular systems. Thus you learn to moderate your sexual impulses. Be open to loving another person. Too much self-love makes you unattractive.

Venus Opposite Ascendant

Love affairs are your stock in trade. You are physically attractive. Women around you contribute to your sense of beauty. Sometimes you are strongly attracted to wasteful, indulgent people who seek only pleasure and not a lasting relationship.

Mars Sextile Jupiter

You have immense willpower to apply to business propositions. You desire freedom. You have many opportunities to direct your energy into specific activities. Sometimes you miss romantic relationships because you are too busy pursuing other interests.

Mars Biquintile Uranus

When you focus on physical pleasure, you have nearly inexhaustible reserves of energy. Yet you appreciate the rhythm of sexual excitement and acknowledge your partner's and your own limits. Use your creative skills to develop the openness and trust necessary for complete surrender.

Mars Opposite Ascendant

You can be argumentative and even violent. Leave these two qualities outside the bedroom door—always.

The Mental Side of Sex (Yes, There Is a Mental Side)

We are intelligent, thinking beings. We thrive in situations where we can apply our critical thinking to problems. Even in the arenas of romance and sexuality, thinking through our feelings can be helpful. Your approach to thinking about sexuality may be different from that of your partner, and it's good to understand those differences.

Mercury in Taurus

You are adept at formal thinking and logic. You understand the practical application of logic and take a deliberate approach to most activities. You tend to be somewhat one-sided in your thinking. Where sexuality is concerned, you benefit both from thinking through what you really want, and from opening your mind to new possibilities. This doesn't mean you have to try everything you hear or read about. It does mean that communication with your partner can expand the range of sexual pleasure in your relationship.

Mercury in the Eighth House

You can be sharply critical. This will shut down your partner's sexual response like nothing else. There is no place for sarcasm where physical pleasure is concerned. You are better off discussing your preferences ahead of time and listening to your partner's desires. Then you can enjoy sexuality without argument or back talk.

Mercury Semisextile Venus

You have a keen sense of form, and therefore "design" your sex life artistically. There is a lighthearted quality to your passion.

Mercury Square Saturn

Shyness or narrow-mindedness can prevent you from achieving the highest physical satisfaction. In fact, these attitudes can actually interfere with the nervous system, preventing transmittal of physical sensations. You can enhance sexuality in two ways. Cultivate longer-term relationships to overcome shyness naturally, and broaden your thinking through reading, conversations with trusted friends, and even experimentation.

Mercury Opposite Uranus

Intuition plays a role in your sex life. Pay attention to subtle yet revealing clues about your partner. Then ask questions to explore your insights. Be truthful, but not so blunt that you cause hurt feelings.

Mercury Biquintile Neptune

You enhance your sexual experience when you allow yourself to go deep within the imaginative sphere. You probably see fireworks when the sex is great. You identify subtle connections with your partner, and anchor them with a touch or a word.

Mercury Quincunx Pluto

You get into and out of relationships very quickly. The same goes for getting into and out of bed. Harness your powers of suggestion. Plan sexual encounters, and adjust the plan to suit your partner's needs and desires of the moment.

Mercury Sextile Midheaven

Reflecting on previous physical encounters can be useful, but only if it is reflection, and not obsession. As you mentally log your successes, you build a base for future sexual success. Remember, it works well to tell your partner what you want, just as it helps when you ask what he or she needs.

Mercury Quincunx Ascendant

You are sharply attuned to any signals coming through your sense organs. Adjust every area of sensual input to enhance sexual pleasure. Check with your partner to discover different tastes in music, scent, food, and touch to enhance your pleasure. Your favorite dancing music may not work in bed.

Your Emotional Needs Seen Through an Astrological Lens

Emotions play a huge role in sexuality. If you have ever been unable to engage in sex because of your emotions, you know this. By understanding the emotional differences between you and your partner, you take a giant step toward greater physical satisfaction.

Moon in Virgo

You need to understand the intimate details of sex. Even in the midst of a passionate moment, you are considering the practical aspects of the situation. Your approach to sex is somewhat methodical, and you love a tidy environment. Take care of the neatness details ahead of time, and have everything you will want or need available. Then allow yourself to explore new ways to pleasure your partner—and yourself. Hint: learn to relax your mind and enjoy the details of physical sensation. For you, sex without love and respect is a pale imitation of the real thing.

Moon in the Twelfth House

Two things are essential for your sexual pleasure: privacy and more privacy. You are not one to put your sex life on display. Oh, you may dress for passion, but when the moment comes, it had better be in a safe, secure, private environment. Then you can really let your hair down. Not one to kiss and tell, you expect the same from your partner.

Moon Square Neptune

The subconscious plays a big role in your fantasy life, and therefore in successful physical encounters. Allow your mind to run wild as you create a wildly passionate setting. Incorporate details from what you know about your partner. A favorite essential oil scent can work sexual wonders.

Moon Semisextile North Node

Living with your sexual partner is a requirement. Flings do not enhance your sexual satisfaction. Even when you are living together, it takes time for you to adapt to your partner's quirks. Allow time for the relationship to deepen. Then you get the very best sex possible.

Moon Quintile Midheaven

Your spiritual values are profoundly important to you. Create peace, and you will enrich both your spiritual awareness and your physical pleasure.

Spiritual Ecstasy Through Physical Relationships

As you cultivate your relationship and establish a deeper connection with your partner, you will find that you achieve higher and higher levels of physical satisfaction. In addition, your spiritual connection is developing. Knowing each other spiritually enhances physical satisfaction immeasurably.

Neptune in Sagittarius

You are often able to foresee outcomes. Applied to your sex life, this skill has a deepening effect. You make fewer errors in judgment as you get to know your partner better. Use your intuition, and then ask your partner—it's always good to confirm a fantasy before you get too deep into playing it out. Now here's the tricky part: you need to examine your partner's fantasies the same way. This requires an excellent level of verbal communication between you.

Neptune in the Third House

Because you are impressionable, you absorb energy from your sexual partner. It's imperative that the two of you have open communication to avoid misunderstandings about the source or direction of your partner's emotions. It's possible they are not directed toward you at all. Your mystical tendencies can become a significant facet of your sex life when you cultivate shared ecstatic experiences of all kinds, sex included.

Neptune Sextile Pluto

This aspect is shared by entire generations of people, so your partner is very likely to have it in the birth chart too. You have an interest in mystical and supernatural phenomena. This interest can enhance your sex life when you apply what you know about your inner life to your sexual partnership. You may decide to explore extraordinary sexual possibilities. You may instead come to see your sex life as a significant part of your spiritual life, and vice versa.

Self and Other in Intimate Partnership

The perception of self and other becomes blurred in sexual relationships. The desire to merge becomes all powerful, and then ebbs as the desire to be independent takes over. This ebb and flow of sexual energy makes for excitement in intimate relationships. Even if you are not actively engaging in sex, you can feel the tides of emotional attachment between you.

Ascendant in Libra

Generally you are affectionate and pleasant with your partner. Even in your physical relationship you usually exhibit good manners. Problem: you don't like anything that even resembles dirty work. If you are overly fastidious where sex is concerned, you won't be able to enjoy the passion of the moment. In addition, you can't depend on your partner to make all the moves or come up with all the new ideas. It's very important for you to focus your attentions on one partner at a time. The depth of passion grows for you as you develop a sense of loyalty within the relationship.

Descendant in Aries

Your sexual partner tends to be restless when things are too calm. Your sexual relationship thrives when you consider new possibilities and at least try things your partner suggests. Your partner is likely to be more impulsive than you, willing to jump in the sack at the slightest hint. If you disagree strongly, there could be angry fireworks. When the two of you agree, all the fire is concentrated in your physical relationship. How much better is that?

The Role of Self-Awareness in Sexuality

Know Thyself. This axiom has stood the test of time in every arena. Now you have information to help you understand your own sexual attitudes, desires, likes, and dislikes. As you listen to your inner urges, and communicate them to your partner, you find that the two of you are more willing partners.

Midheaven in Cancer

You wish to establish yourself as an individual in the world, and you may do this in your sex life by holding back something from your partner. This is not a matter of not loving your partner. It's about your desire for independence.

Deep within you is a well of self-confidence that has developed over years of experience. You have the capacity to work and keep working toward personal goals. What does this have to do with your sex life? Everything. Bottom line: you don't expect peak sexual satisfaction from the start. You are willing to apply energy and time to creating intense passion in your relationship.

Do You Have Sexual Karma?

Each of us has some karma to work out in the sexual arena. Intimate relationships help us by revealing our weaknesses and flaws, but also by showing where our greatest glory can be found. When dealing with a partner, it's important to realize that your karmas may collide, but they are not identical.

North Node in the First House

One of your biggest challenges is to accept your partner not as a reflection of yourself, but as part of yourself. You may seek a partner who will fulfill a sexual role that is a projection of your own fantasies. The partner is almost doomed to failure because your fantasies are constantly changing. Only the most unusual partner can keep up. In addition, your partner has his or her own agenda at work, and those fantasies may not mesh easily with yours.

Your challenge in any relationship is to express your fantasies verbally. Then when your fantasy shifts, your partner knows immediately. This may cause friction at first, but in the long run, passion will increase as the two of you share your deepest private desires.

North Node in Libra

While your partner is linear and direct, you seek balance. The linear approach can take you way out on a limb with your emotions, a place where you may be intensely uncomfortable. After all, sexual completion is about orgasm, and orgasm can feel very out of balance. Your karma involves experiencing extremes of passion, while also preserving a sense of balance. In the past you have been the one who was assertive, or perhaps even aggressive, in sexual encounters. As the recipient of your partner's aggression, you now must learn to accept what you can, communicate about your insecurities, and develop trust in your partner.

Conclusion

If you are reading this, you have probably gathered that I believe your sex life will benefit from the development of long-term relationships in which both partners are committed to the success of the relationship. While the initial flush of magnetic attraction and sexual passion will get you into a relationship, sustained attention and effort will raise your experience to the level of sheer ecstasy.

You have no doubt encountered contradictions in this material. These provide you with food for thought. How do you experience those contradictions in your sex life? Do they cause problems or add interest? As you and your partner explore sexuality together, you will resolve the contradictions within yourself and provide the greatest pleasure for your partner.

Comparison of the Partners' Charts

I have charted a simple comparison of each part of these two interpretations to show how differences and similarities work together. I have compared similar factors in both charts.

For the sake of comparison, I have noted the compatibility of each pair of factors with "yes" or "no." In real life we are adaptable—a firm no today can become a yes tomorrow, and vice versa. You will also find areas of compatibility based on different astrological factors that reflect similar feelings. Even when we perceive specific situations very differently, we can usually accommodate others without much stress. When there are many disharmonious factors, then the relationship may become difficult and stressful. On the other hand, when there are no disharmonies, the relationship can become dull and boring. In the list, a yes means that the two factors are generally compatible. A no means a lack of ease or compatibility between the charts. The list is annotated with explanations for some of the factors. That way you can see why there is a dynamic connection, either pleasurable or not.

The table of comparisons provides several kinds of information. First, it shows compatibilities by element, mode, and house. These are some of the most basic astrological indicators. Traditionally fire and air elements are thought to be compatible, as are earth and water. The modes—the three modes of action—are less compatible with each other, although mutable chart factors are somewhat compatible with cardinal and fixed because of the flexible nature of the mutable signs. House compatibility is related to the number of signs between houses. If the house numbers add up to an odd number, they are thought to be less compatible, while those adding up to an even number are considered more compatible.

A second way of evaluating the data is to look at cases where the same two planets are in aspect. The list includes explanations of the "yes" and "no" indicators. If the aspects are the same, or if both aspects are constructive, there is a high level of compatibility. If the aspects are both challenging, then there is some compatibility because both people have to face similar challenges. If one aspect is constructive and the other challenging, then the two people experience similar input in very different ways, and therefore there is less compatibility. When one person has an aspect and the other does not, there may be a lack of interest or understanding on one side.

A third way of comparing charts considers situations in which a planet is heavily emphasized in one chart through multiple aspects, and relatively unemphasized in the other chart. This means that one partner has a high degree of activity around the energy of a planet, reflected as greater concern in an area of life, while the other partner is directing attention to other areas of life. When this happens, it can mean that the two people are simply interested in very different things.

Astrological Factor	April 29 Birthday	February 1 Birthday	Can They Relate Easily?
Sun Element	Earth—comfort zone is sensual stuff.	Air—comfort zone is the mental.	No. For this to work, either the earth person has to get into the communicative space (talk to the partner), or the air person has to get into the sensual mode (such as giving the partner a back rub).
Sun Mode	Fixed	Fixed	Yes. Both people will tend to be stable and reliable.
Sun Sign	Taurus	Aquarius	No. Earth and air don't blend easily, because earth is more practical and physical, while air is more imaginative and mental.
Sun House	Eighth	Third	No. Remember, when the house numbers add up to an odd number, the energies are "at odds."

Astrological Factor	April 29 Birthday	February 1 Birthday	Can They Relate Easily?
Sun Aspects	Conjunct Mercury	Conjunct Mercury	Yes. Both people tend to think and communicate in the same style, even if the planets are in different signs.
	Semisextile Venus	Semisquare Venus	No. Different social impulses, one toward personal growth, and the other toward stress.
	No Mars aspect	Square Mars	The second person has a higher energy level.
	Semisextile Jupiter	Trine Jupiter	Yes. Similar personal philosophies.
	Square Saturn	No Saturn aspect	The first person has a stronger sense of responsibility.
	Opposition Uranus	No Uranus aspect	The first person has greater intuitive awareness.
	Biquintile Neptune	Quintile Neptune	Yes. Talents and creative impulses run in much the same direction.
	Quincunx Pluto	Sesquisquare Pluto	No, although both represent internalized power urges. They tend to go in different directions, one toward adjusting, and the other toward stressing out over issues.

Astrological Factor	April 29 Birthday	February 1 Birthday	Can They Relate Easily?
Sun Aspects	Sextile Midheaven	No Midheaven aspect	The first person has more opportunities in life to learn about himself or herself.
	Quincunx Ascendant	Square Ascendant	No. The tendency to adjust clashes with the tendency to challenge, and produces a one-sided relationship where one partner does all the adjusting.
Venus Element	Fire	Water	No. Fire and water don't blend easily.
Venus Mode	Cardinal	Mutable	Somewhat.
Venus Sign	Aries	Pisces	No, although there is a natural transition between adjacent signs.
Venus House	Sixth	Fifth	No. The houses are at odds.
Venus Aspects	Conjunct Mars	No Mars aspect	The first person has greater physical passion, but less tenderness.
	Sextile Jupiter	Opposition Jupiter	No. They have different social philosophies.
	Trine Saturn	No Saturn aspect	The first person has greater social sensitivity and enjoys group activities more.
	Quincunx Uranus	Trine Uranus	No. They have different intuitive directions.

Astrological Factor	April 29 Birthday	February 1 Birthday	Can They Relate Easily?
Venus Aspects	No Neptune aspect	Trine Neptune	The second person has more erotic imagination.
	Opposition Pluto	Opposition Pluto	Yes. They have similar views about power in the social sphere.
	No North Node aspect	Conjunct North Node	The second person has more interest in romance.
	Square Midheaven	Biquintile Midheaven	No. Self-awareness takes them in different directions.
	Opposition Ascendant	Sesquisquare Ascendant	Somewhat. Similar response to social tensions.
Mars Sign	Aries	Scorpio	No, but both are fiery sexual partners.
Mars House	Sixth	First	No. The houses are at odds.
Mars Aspects	Sextile Jupiter	Semisquare Jupiter	No. One partner is always seeing opportunities, while the other tends to feel hemmed in.
	No Saturn aspect	Quincunx Saturn	The second person faces more adjustments in life regarding career and physical injury.
	Biquintile Uranus	Semisquare Uranus	No. Creative thinking and internal stress take the partners in different directions with their thinking.
	No North Node aspect	Sesquisquare North Node	The second person tends to quarrel more with groups and associates.

Astrological Factor	April 29 Birthday	February 1 Birthday	Can They Relate Easily?
Mars Aspects	Opposition Ascendant	Conjunct Ascendant	No. One partner is projecting feelings, while the other is enjoying the spotlight.
Mercury Sign	Taurus	Aquarius	No, although both have stable energy reserves.
Mercury House	Eighth	Third	No. The houses are at odds.
Mercury Aspects	Semisextile Venus	No Venus aspect	The first person talks more about love.
	No Jupiter aspect	Trine Jupiter	The second person talks more about business and practical things.
	Square Saturn	Quintile Saturn	No. Life challenges slow the first person down in an area where the second person is creative.
	Opposition Uranus	Trine Uranus	No, unless both partners are skilled in using their intuition.
	Biquintile Neptune	No Neptune aspect	The first person talks more about fantasies.
	Quincunx Pluto	No Pluto aspect	The first person tries harder to persuade the partner.
	No North Node aspect	Sextile North Node	The second person has more friends and business contacts.

Astrological Factor	April 29 Birthday	February 1 Birthday	Can They Relate Easily?
Mercury Aspects	Sextile Midheaven	No Midheaven aspect	The first person is more self-aware.
	Quincunx Ascendant	No Ascendant aspect	The first person enjoys exchanging ideas more.
Moon Sign	Virgo	Cancer	Yes.
Moon House	Twelfth	Ninth	No. The houses are at odds.
Moon Aspects	No Mercury aspect	Opposition Mercury	The second person is more sensitive to criticism.
	No Venus aspect	Trine Venus	The second person has deeper feelings of love and tenderness.
	No Uranus aspect	Sextile Uranus	The second person feels greater emotional tension.
	Square Neptune	Trine Neptune	No. One partner sees obstacles where the other sees opportunities.
	No Pluto aspect	Sextile Pluto	The second person has more explosive outbursts of feelings.
	Semisextile North Node	Trine North Node	Yes. Both seek emotionally satisfying relationships.
	Quintile Midheaven	Semisextile Midheaven	Yes. Both seek greater self-understanding.
Neptune Sign	Sagittarius	Scorpio	No. The signs are at odds.
Neptune House	Third	First	Yes. The partners are supportive of each other's dreams.

Astrological Factor	April 29 Birthday	February 1 Birthday	Can They Relate Easily?
Neptune Aspects	Sextile Pluto	Sextile Pluto	Yes. They share an interest in the supernatural.
	No North Node aspect	Trine North Node	The second person may expect too much of other people.
	No Midheaven aspect	Square Midheaven	The second person has less self-confidence and is less goal-oriented.
Ascendant/ Descendant	Libra Ascendant/ Aries Descendant	Scorpio Ascendant/ Taurus Descendant	No. The signs are at odds.
Midheaven/IC	Cancer Midheaven/ Capricorn IC	Leo Midheaven/ Aquarius IC	No. The signs are at odds.
North Node House	First	Fifth	Yes. The partners are supportive of each other's desire to have good relationships with friends and business associates.
North Node Sign	Libra	Aries	No. Each has the flip side of the other's karma. Both have to work at accepting each other's point of view.

Evaluation

Making a straight comparison of like factors in our two example charts, we find eleven yes factors and twenty-seven no factors, for a ratio of 1 to 2.7. This is not very promising, as there are nearly three times as many areas of disagreement where the sex life is concerned. Imagine yourself disagreeing with your sexual partner two times out of every three. That wouldn't feel warm, cozy, and safe.

In addition, there are twenty-four aspects on the list that occur in only one of the charts. These are indicators of individual interests that have some impact on the sex life, but less than the mutual aspects. They reflect areas of life that can satisfy each individual outside the sexual relationship.

For the sake of illustration, I made a comparison between Paul Newman and Joanne Woodward. I found twice as many nos as yeses, with four additional factors indicating some degree of agreement. This still does not seem ideal, yet we know their relationship has lasted for many years and appears to be quite strong. It is likely that much of their compatibility lies in areas other than sex.

In comparing the charts of Bill and Hillary Clinton, I found the most striking difference between Neptune aspects in their charts. Hillary has only three Neptune aspects, all in the opportunity and creative sphere. Bill has eight Neptune aspects, with all but two either a conjunction or a constructive aspect. Bill and Hillary share the Neptune-sextile-Pluto aspect with everyone in their generation. Not counting that combination, the closest connection to Neptune in their charts is Mars.

The large difference in the number of Neptune aspects tells us that Bill is more idealistic in his thinking, and less practical. He has eight ways to use his ability to create illusion, for himself and for others. He deluded himself into thinking that sex with an intern was appropriate behavior, that he would never get caught, that Hillary would be all right with it, etc. He thought he could control the situation by lying. He was wrong. His sexual misconduct caused public disgrace and could easily have cost him his marriage. His lying could have even cost him the presidency.

Hillary is not so impractical. She was furious, but didn't go off the deep end in anger. She understands the power in their partnership, and wants to preserve it. So far they make a public show of staying together. We of course don't know what their private life is like, so we can't evaluate the impact of Bill's sexual indiscretions in that regard. We can also surmise that, like Newman and Woodward, there is a lot more to this relationship than sex. They may stay together for an entirely different set of reasons, their daughter not the least of them.

I also compared the charts of two people whom I know have a mutually satisfying sexual relationship. In this example the yes and no factors are nearly equal (ten and eleven), and there are eight additional factors indicating some degree of agreement. This is a more desirable balance of energies between two charts. The charts show, at this very basic level, a high level of agreement. Still, there are eleven ways to disagree, if they are so inclined.

Summary

When you use astrology to evaluate a sexual relationship, you have a unique perspective. Not all sexual relationships are based on the same emotional, material, and spiritual needs. This means that what works for you might or might not work for me. This book and CD-ROM are designed to evaluate the potential. It's up to the partners to make sense of the evaluation in terms of their own goals and desires.

Conclusion
How to Make the Most of What You Have

In the beginning of a relationship when the physical attraction is most passionate, you can build sexual compatibility by exploring areas where you agree about what brings pleasure. You can each learn successful ways to offer pleasure. Considering that most relationships involve a partner of the opposite sex, there are bound to be different sexual needs and desires. Same-sex partners have the advantage of knowing firsthand what is likely to please the partner on the physical level.

When you prepare charts and compare your partner's chart and interpretation to your own, keep these factors in mind:

- The list of factors is only a list. It is not a rigid measurement or evaluation.
- Some people can tolerate higher levels of stress or pain, and therefore may enjoy a bit of pain along with sex.
- Some very strong relationships are based upon factors other than sex. Those factors contribute to sexual enjoyment in unique ways. For example, if you and your partner are both powerful figures in your professions, you both may experience a sense of power in the bedroom too. This means you don't have to tiptoe around each other where sex is concerned.

- Some people like a great deal of foreplay. This can include delicious food, suitable ambiance, music, dancing, and conversation. If all those areas go well, then sexual pleasure will very likely be increased. You can use your areas of agreement and disagreement to shape the foreplay.

- If the two charts contain similar aspects, or even the same number of aspects to specific planets, this indicates that you and your partner are focusing on the same areas of life, but in different ways. For instance, in the example charts in chapter 16, both partners have seven aspects to Venus. This indicates that they both concentrate on issues of physical beauty, harmonious interchange of energy, and mutual social interests. They therefore are likely to enjoy similar sports and social activities.

   In contrast, one partner has three aspects to the Moon and the other partner has seven. The partner with seven Moon aspects is more focused on emotional issues. These two would have to work through some emotional baggage to find the lingerie! Emotions are an integral part of satisfying sexual activity. These two would need to take special care to create a safe emotional atmosphere for their sex life. The partner with fewer Moon aspects must pay close attention to the partner's emotional responses, being careful never to dismiss or ridicule the partner.

What should you do about differences or discord? How do you resolve a few issues? What do you do if you have lots of issues? You can work on each area. First of all, if your partner does something that causes you pain, let him or her know right away. A loving partner will not intentionally hurt you (unless that is part of the excitement you both agree upon). You can choose nonsexual, nonthreatening situations to discuss sexual differences. You can agree to forego certain techniques or postures that don't provide pleasure for both partners. Or you can agree to soften any hard-edged sexuality—compromise rather than refuse altogether.

Perhaps the best use of the interpretation program is to investigate how you tick sexually, and to discover the same about your partner. Physical pleasure is not a contest, so the scores on the comparison are really not the point. Understanding your own desires is the place to start. If you understand what you want on both the conscious and unconscious levels, you are far more likely to get it. Recognizing your partner's desires and needs comes next. It's a mistake to assume that your partner wants exactly what you want in the sexual satisfaction department. Getting a picture of his or her physical focus through astrology can help you create the best possible sex life for both of you.

Appendix 1

Step-by-Step Guide
to Mapping Your Sex Life

This guide follows the same outline as the example in chapter 16. As you compare your chart to your partner's chart, fill in the blanks for aspects and other factors in the two charts. Then read the aspect section in chapter 15 to see what each aspect indicates, and how the two of you "mesh" sexually.

Astrological Factor	First Person's Birthday	Second Person's Birthday	Can They Relate Easily?
Sun Element			
Sun Mode			
Sun Sign			
Sun House			

Astrological Factor	First Person's Birthday	Second Person's Birthday	Can They Relate Easily?
Sun Aspects			
Venus Element			
Venus Mode			
Venus Sign			
Venus House			
Venus Aspects			

Astrological Factor	First Person's Birthday	Second Person's Birthday	Can They Relate Easily?
Mars Sign			
Mars House			
Mars Aspects			
Mercury Sign			
Mercury House			
Mercury Aspects			

Astrological Factor	First Person's Birthday	Second Person's Birthday	Can They Relate Easily?
Moon Sign			
Moon House			
Moon Aspects			
Neptune Sign			
Neptune House			
Neptune Aspects			

Astrological Factor	First Person's Birthday	Second Person's Birthday	Can They Relate Easily?
Ascendant/ Descendant			
Midheaven/IC			
North Node House			
North Node Sign			

Appendix 2

Map Your Sex Life
Using the CD-ROM

First you need to install the program. Just remove the CD-ROM from its folder, and place it in your computer's CD-ROM drive. The program will begin to install itself.

If it does not start automatically, click on the Start menu and select "Run." In the Run menu dialog box, type in your corresponding CD-ROM drive followed by the file name SETUP.exe. Typically, the CD-ROM is set up as D:\. The install wizard will run and guide you through the rest of the process.

For an alternate method, you can access your CD-ROM drive by clicking on "My Computer" and then the CD-ROM drive (typically D:\). Double-click on the SETUP.exe icon.

You will see a screen called "Mapping Your Sex Life," which is pictured on the following page.

Mapping Your Sex Life is a basic astrology program, designed around the most sophisticated astrology programming available. Cosmic Patterns, in collaboration with Llewellyn Worldwide, has developed this program to provide you with birth charts (the circle with all the astrological symbols) and interpretations of those charts (eight- to ten-page printouts of information about your approach to intimacy and passion).

Let's discuss the choices you have on this screen:

- The Start menu is used to create a chart.
- The About menu provides information about Llewellyn Worldwide, the publisher of *Mapping Your Sex Life,* and Cosmic Patterns Software, the designer of the program.
- The Quit menu allows you to exit from the program.

Creating an Astrology Chart and Interpretation

To use your program, click on the Start menu at the top of the screen and select "New List of Charts (New Session)." If you are returning to the program and want to see the last chart you made, select "Continue with Charts of Previous Session."

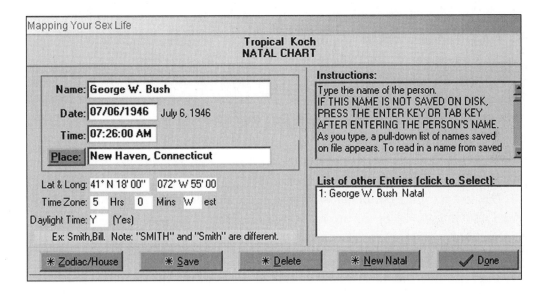

This is where you enter your birth information. There are some simple instructions on the right side of the screen, similar to what follows here. Let's make a birth chart for Mata Hari as an example. She was born on August 7, 1876, at 1:00 PM LMT in Leeuwarden, Netherlands.

- In the Name box, type "Mata Hari," and Enter.
- In the Date box, type "08071876", and Enter. (Always enter the date in mm dd yyyy format.)
- In the Time field, type "010000 PM" (the birth time in hh mm ss format), and Enter.
- In the Place box, type "Leeuwarden, Netherlands" (the birth place). As soon as you begin typing, a list will drop down. You will see Leeuwarden in the list. Select it. The drop-down list will disappear, and you will see Leeuwarden, Netherlands,

in the Place box. You will also see information filled in the boxes below it: the latitude is 53N12 00, the longitude is 005E46 00, the time zone is 0 hours 0 minutes West, and the Daylight Saving Time box is marked "L." The "L" indicates that at the time Mata Hari was born, the Netherlands was observing Local Mean Time. You will typically see "Y" or "N" in this box, indicating yes or no.

If your city does not automatically come up in the list, you can use a nearby city from the list. You can also look up your birth place in an atlas to find the latitude and longitude, time zone, and daylight saving time, and fill in this information. Generally, a city close to the birth place is close enough for most purposes and will also be in the same time zone. If the time zone information is different, your chart could be off by an hour one way or the other. Depending on the distance your choice is from your actual birth place, your chart will be slightly different. You can obtain the correct longitude, latitude, and time information from a timetable book for astrology. Two atlases are listed in the bibliography of this book.

The Zodiac/House button allows you to select a different house system. This program automatically selects the tropical zodiac and Koch house system. Experiment with the other choices to see what changes on the chart wheel. In this program the interpretation will change only if you select the sidereal zodiac.

Select the "Save" button at the bottom of the screen to save the chart (you can delete it later if you need to), and then click "OK."

Then select the "Done" button. If you forget to save and go directly to the Done button, you will get a prompt asking if you want to save the data. In fact, all the way along prompts appear to help you enter the data.

The screen pictured on the next page is what you will see next.

```
                The Mapping Your Sex Life Report for


                        George W. Bush

                          July 6, 1946

                           7:26 AM

                     New Haven, Connecticut




     Calculated for:
     Time Zone 5 hours West
     Latitude: 41 N 18
     Longitude: 72 W 55
     Tropical Zodiac, Daylight Savings Time observed.


     Positions of Planets at Birth:
     Sun      position  is  13 deg.  47 min.  of  Cancer
     Moon     position  is  16 deg.  42 min.  of  Libra
     Mercury  position  is   9 deg.  50 min.  of  Leo
     Venus    position  is  21 deg.  30 min.  of  Leo
     Mars     position  is   9 deg.  18 min.  of  Virgo
```

You will see Mata Hari's name and birth data, plus more information lists, and finally the interpretation. To print this interpretation, click on the Print menu and select "Print."

If you select "Wheel" from the Reports menu, a chart form will appear. At the upper left corner it is labeled "Wheel Style FAC." This form should look just like the one pictured here.

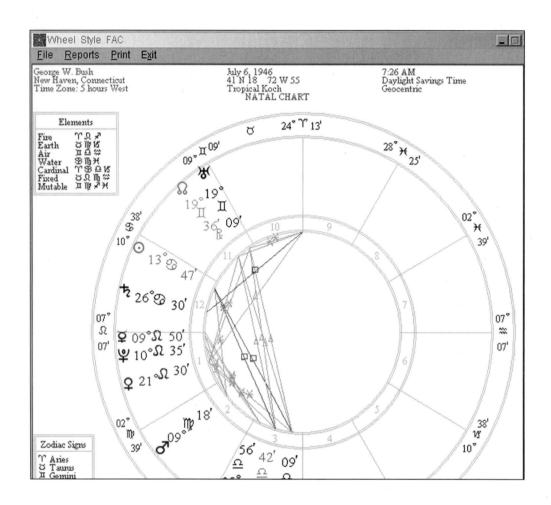

To print the chart, click on the Print menu and select "Print."

To go back to the opening screen, click on the Exit menu and select "Yes: Exit to Opening Screen." From here you can either exit the program by clicking on the Quit menu and selecting "Yes," or you can click on the Start menu to make another chart and interpretation.

That's it! You can now create charts and interpretations for any birth information you want. This program is so easy to use that you won't need much help.

Suggested Reading List

The American Atlas: U.S. Latitudes and Longitudes, Time Changes and Time Zones. Compiled and programmed by Neil F. Michelsen. San Diego, CA: ACS Publications, 1978.

Ashman, Bernie. *SignMates*. St. Paul, MN: Llewellyn Publications, 2000.

Bennet, E. A. *What Jung Really Said*. New York: Schocken Books, 1967.

Burk, Kevin. *Astrology*. St. Paul, MN: Llewellyn Publications, 2001.

Fairfield, Gail. *Choice Centered Astrology*. York Beach, ME: Weiser, 1998.

Green, Jeffrey Wolf. *Pluto, Vol II: The Soul's Evolution Through Relationships*. St. Paul, MN: Llewellyn Publications, 2000.

The International Atlas: World Latitudes, Longitudes and Time Changes. Compiled and programmed by Thomas G. Shanks. San Diego, CA: ACS Publications, 1985.

Pond, David. *Astrology & Relationships*. St. Paul, MN: Llewellyn Publications, 2001.

———. *Mapping Your Romantic Relationships*. St. Paul, MN: Llewellyn Publications, 2004.

Rakela, Christine. *The Love Relationship Formula*. St. Paul, MN: Llewellyn Publications, 2004.

Riske, Kris Brandt, M.A. *Mapping Your Future*. St. Paul, MN: Llewellyn Publications, 2004.

Glossary

Ascendant (rising sign)—The degree and sign of the zodiac that was visible at the eastern horizon at the time of birth. The cusp of the First House. The Ascendant reflects the individual's personality and physical characteristics.

Aspects—Relationships between points in the chart. They are angles measured from the center of the chart. Specific angles are found to be significant:

Conjunction (0 degrees)—Planets that are together in the zodiac. Indicates prominence of the two energies.

Semisextile (30 degrees)—Planets that are exactly one sign apart on the zodiac. Indicates growth; can be uncomfortable.

Semisquare (45 degrees)—Planets exactly one and a half signs apart in the zodiac. Indicates internal tension and stress.

Sextile (60 degrees)—Planets that are two signs apart are able to cooperate to produce opportunities.

Quintile (72 degrees)—Planets separated by one-fifth of the zodiac contribute creatively to each other.

Square (90 degrees)—Planets three signs apart indicate challenges.

Trine (120 degrees)—Planets four signs apart indicate comfortable conditions where their energies are concerned.

Sesquisquare, or sesquiquadrate (135 degrees)—Planets four and a half signs apart indicate agitation, which may not be evident to observers.

Biquintile (144 degrees)—Planets separated by two-fifths of the zodiac indicate the quality of inborn talents.

Quincunx, or inconjunct (150 degrees)—Planets five signs apart indicate the nature of adjustments the individual will be required to make.

Opposition (180 degrees)—Planets opposite each other in the zodiac indicate where the individual will be aware of differences.

Detriment—The sign opposite the sign of rulership. Planets in their sign of detriment reach their best expression only after much work on the part of the individual.

Dignity—A classical astrology term used to indicate the degree of comfort, or the power, of a planet in a particular sign.

Elements—Four designations of principal characteristics of all matter and life:

Fire signs—Energetic, active, impulsive. The fire signs are Aries, Leo, and Sagittarius.

Earth signs—Practical, dependable, conservative. The earth signs are Taurus, Virgo, and Capricorn.

Air signs—Mental, versatile, detached. The airs signs are Gemini, Libra, and Aquarius.

Water signs—Emotional, imaginative, impressionable. The water signs are Cancer, Scorpio, and Pisces.

Exaltation—A classical astrology term for the sign or house where a planet is capable of its best expression, with the possible exception of domicile (the house or sign the planet rules.

Fall—The sign opposite the sign of exaltation. This is a sign where the planet's energy tends to "fall away" from the highest or best expression.

Karma—Conditions brought about through cause-and-effect relationships. We experience karma in the present, based on our past actions, and we accumulate future karma through our actions in the present.

Midheaven—The degree and sign of the zodiac that was in the highest point of the sky at the birth time. The Midheaven is on the ecliptic, and is at the point where the meridian intersects the ecliptic. The meridian is a great circle that intersects the North and South Poles, and also is directly overhead at the place of birth.

Modes (or qualities, quadruplicities)—Three ways in which individuals express themselves through their thoughts and actions:

    Cardinal—Assertive, ambitious, impatient. The cardinal signs are Aries, Cancer, Libra, and Capricorn.

    Fixed—Stable, consistent, patient. The fixed signs are Taurus, Leo, Scorpio, and Aquarius.

    Mutable (common)—Adaptable, responsive, restless. The mutable signs are Gemini, Virgo, Sagittarius, and Pisces.

Psychological types—A method developed by Carl Jung to describe four basic ways that people approach life:

    Sensation—The capacity to relate to the world primarily through the five senses.

    Thinking—The capacity to recognize the purpose or meaning of what we sense.

    Intuition—The capacity to project possibilities into the future.

    Feeling—The capacity to determine the value of what we perceive.

Retrograde motion—The apparent change in direction of a planet. Periodically the planets appear to move backward in the sky from our perspective. Retrograde motion, as perceived from the earth, occurs because of the relative speed of the earth and other planets, and because of their positions relative to each other.

Rulership—The association of a planet with a specific house or sign.

Saturn (or other planet) Return—The time when a planet has moved forward in the zodiac (transited) to the same degree it held in the birth chart. These times are significant because the planet's energy is most aligned with the individual's energy when it is in that degree.

Synastry—The comparison of two charts in order to determine compatibility in a relationship.

Index

To Write to the Author

If you wish to contact the author or would like more information about this book, please write to the author in care of Llewellyn Worldwide, and we will forward your request. Both the author and publisher appreciate hearing from you and learning of your enjoyment of this book and how it has helped you. Llewellyn Worldwide cannot guarantee that every letter written to the author can be answered, but all will be forwarded. Please write to:

Stephanie Jean Clement, Ph.D.
℅ Llewellyn Worldwide
P.O. Box 64383, Dept. 0-7387-0644-2
St. Paul, MN 55164-0383, U.S.A.

Please enclose a self-addressed, stamped envelope for reply,
or $1.00 to cover costs. If outside U.S.A., enclose
international postal reply coupon.

Many of Llewellyn's authors have websites with additional information and resources. For more information, please visit our website at
http://www.llewellyn.com.

LLEWELLYN ORDERING INFORMATION

Order Online:
Visit our website at www.llewellyn.com, select your books, and order them on our secure server.

Order by Phone:
- Call toll-free within the U.S. at 1-877-NEW-WRLD (1-877-639-9753). Call toll-free within Canada at 1-866-NEW-WRLD (1-866-639-9753)
- We accept VISA, MasterCard, and American Express

Order by Mail:
Send the full price of your order (MN residents add 7% sales tax) in U.S. funds, plus postage & handling to:

Llewellyn Worldwide
P.O. Box 64383, Dept. 0-7387-0644-2
St. Paul, MN 55164-0383, U.S.A.

Postage & Handling:

Standard (U.S., Mexico, & Canada). If your order is:
$49.99 and under, add $3.00
$50.00 and over, FREE STANDARD SHIPPING

AK, HI, PR: $15.00 for one book plus $1.00 for each additional book.

International Orders (airmail only):
$16.00 for one book plus $3.00 for each additional book

Orders are processed within 2 business days. Please allow for normal shipping time.
Postage and handling rates subject to change.

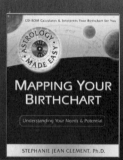

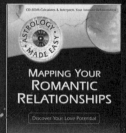